Masonic Research Lodges, Bodies, and Societies

Masonic Research Lodges, Bodies, and Societies

2021-2024 Edition

KEN JP STUCZYNSKI

CYPHRGLYFFE, AN IMPRINT OF AMORPHOUS
PUBLISHING GUILD
BUFFALO, NY USA

To all who travel in
foreign lands ...
be they geographic,
intellectual, or spiritual

Contents

Chapters, Councils, and Priories

Research Societies and Other Organizations

Online Resources

Foreword

One of the fun things about visiting a Masonic lodge is discovering some special "something" that ties them all together in addition to Freemasonry. Such lodges are known as "affinity lodges." For example, Ye Olde Cups and Balls Lodge, California, is so new, it's still working "Under Dispensation" (U.D.). Its members are magicians. Shotokan Karate Lodge No.9752, England, was formed in 2002, and most of its members are involved in martial arts. One of the most successful and influential affinity lodges is Quatuor Coronati Lodge No.2076, England, formed in 1886. It was the first of what are known as "Research Lodges."

A research lodge primarily exists as a forum to disseminate Masonic knowledge, usually in the form of research papers written by its members and often subsequently published in volumes usually known as transactions. "Ars Quatuor Coronatorum" (AQC), the transactions of the Quatuor Coronati Lodge, have been published annually since 1886. One thing that usually distinguishes papers presented in a research lodge is the meticulous attention to documenting facts. Some of the papers achieve the standards of academic journals. Quatuor Coronati describes itself as "the world's premier Masonic research lodge. Established in 1884 and consecrated in

1886, our founders adopted an evidence-based approach to Masonic history that replaced the more imaginative writings of earlier authors; it became known as the 'authentic school' of Masonic research."

The success of Quatuor Coronati Lodge and AQC have inspired many other research lodges around the world – small and large, formal and casual, but all are inspired by the goal of presenting the story of Freemasonry in a factual and interesting manner. Brother Ken JP Stuczynski has assembled this grand collection of "biographies" of Masonic Research Lodges around the world. And it's not just Masonic Lodges but also Royal Arch Chapters, Cryptic Councils, Templar Priories and Commanderies, Societies, and more. If a group of Masons wants to gather and discuss the history of the Craft, then they will find a way to do it. The organizational details are only incidental, but these details can be later important, and Bro. Stuczynski has tried to preserve as much of this as possible for future researchers.

I can imagine a researcher working on the biography of an important Mason and then coming across this collection. The researcher then realizes there is (or was) a Masonic research group working in the area of the subject of his, and maybe – just maybe – they published something on the topic of his searches. Now there is a new rabbit hole to go down and more libraries to visit and more new friends to make along the way.

Such side trips are the true joy of research and the great value of this book. Enjoy!

S. Brent Morris, PhD

Past Master, Quatuor Coronati Lodge No.2076
Past President, Maryland Masonic Research Society
Former Editor, *Heredom*, "Transactions of the Scottish Rite Research Society"
Former Editor, *The Scottish Rite Journal*

Disclaimer

This book was written independently of any entity mentioned within or any affiliation of the author.

The author makes no claim as to the information herein being definitive or guaranteed against errors and omissions. Effort was given to include every entity that submitted information or had adequate sources. Entities which had more information readily available, or ones more closely known by the author, may be more comprehensive, and ones that do not upkeep their public face and are unavoidably more vague. Corrections submitted to the author will be considered and rectified in future editions or, if egregious in nature, a revision of this edition.

Introduction

Until the late 19th Century, the academic approach of Masonry was imaginative, or more honestly put, unscholarly and disorganized. Even some of what was being written by Mackey and Pike was more fairy tale than historical fact. According to Brother S. Brent Morris, "Pike leaned more toward the romantic" but in the end conceded that Masonry as a continuous tradition was only a few centuries old — not tracing to Solomon, the Pharaohs, and Noah. This shift during Pike's era coincides with the birth of Quatuor Coronati Lodge.

The earliest printed Masonic materials, such as Anderson's Constitutions (1723), and exhortations, such as the famous speech of Chevalier Ramsay (1737), gave us a highly questionable yet unquestioned mythos. Brothers interested in more rigorous (and factual) scholarship, such as Robert Freke Gould and William James Hughan, were among the nine Masons who wished to start a Lodge devoted to an "evidence-based" approach to Masonic history. This later became known as the "Authentic School" of Masonic research. In fact, when Quatuor Coronati began its work, it was joked to be the "Anti-George Oliver Lodge", referring to a fanciful (but not credible) thought leader of the time.

That is where our story begins. Each entry contained

in this book presents an example of a Lodge, society, or subordinate body of a Masonic organization that follows in these footsteps. Within each section – Lodges, Societies, and Other Bodies – they are placed chronologically according to when they were founded. Unless otherwise noted, each of these entities do their work at the time they were researched (2021-2024). Therefore, this book provides a "snapshot" of Masons gathering to do research on things related to, or of interest to, the Fraternity.

Why is this timely?

New generations of Masons are looking for meaning in their lives and not finding it in Freemasonry. It is not that Masonry stopped providing such meaning, but that society's priorities have changed. In much of the 20th Century, at least in America, personal identity was tied to one's livelihood and belonging to organizations of all kinds — churches, social clubs, and sports teams. The measure of one's goodness was charity in the philanthropic, rather than the speculative, etymological sense*.

In the last quarter of a century, membership in all these areas declined greatly. Some falsely blame television, which was around generations previous to this. Some blame the Internet, Social Media, online gaming, streaming entertainment, etc.. There must be some truth to this. After all, you can connect with anyone, any time, without some membership. We have the appearance of belonging without any corresponding obligations or responsibility.

But one may need to be reminded that the book Bowling Alone was published in 2000. This trend predates most of our new excuses. Countless churches are nearly empty at the few services left; recreational establishments such as roller rinks and pool halls are few and far between. We just don't find meaning in crowds like we used to. It takes really special events to fill a theater or stadium. But lest we turn this book into one of sociological analysis, let's just admit this isn't the same world or attitudes that filled our Lodges in the past.

The real question is if Masonry provides anything unique or more than these other groups and activities. If that was so, our demographics would not have been swept out with the same wave. And yet so many Lodges and bodies double down on a bad bet — that what new Brothers join for is another night out of camaraderie. Charitable fundraising is still prevalent, hence the survival of groups such as the Shriners, but one can just as easily subscribe and donate online to a myriad of niche causes. And platforms like GoFundMe have replaced countless benefit events.

The problem isn't that these values, sentiments, and activities are found in the Masonic experience. The problem is that they have been mistaken for its purpose, rather than the means or fruits of it. What we have lost is our soul. Moral instruction has become a haphazard byproduct of the osmosis of ritual. Discussion about life is rarely elevated beyond the temporal and profane. We are concerned primarily with buildings and investments and points of etiquette and tradition. If anyone suggests otherwise, a mountainous body of minutes and photos will rebuke them.

Surely moral instruction is not synonymous with intellectual learning. That is not everyone's personal inclination toward meaning in their lives. But education is a key force upon the vector of one's understanding as a human being. An increase in one's knowledge can be measured by the degree of change within them. So a new question must be asked. Does such education fall under the purview and ability of the Royal Art?

Our ritual alludes strongly to educating oneself in various arts and sciences. We surely do not hand out copies of Vetruvius's *De Architectura* after exposure to columns in the Middle Chamber, but even if taken in the most symbolic sense, for what can all this be a metaphor? What is the meaning of all of it, if not lessons of life itself as iterated time and again in our ritual. *Philosophia est ars vitae* (Lat. "Philosophy is the art of life"). The very meaning of the word "speculative" at the time the ritual was conceived meant philosophical. And in ancient times it was posited that one need study Mathematics (including Geometry) before undertaking the study of life. At the very least, one would think we should bother to know from whence we came (history) and the meanings and allusions of all we experience in our Degrees.

If this were not enough, the (Western) Enlightenment is intimately associated with Freemasonry. Freemasons were among the founders of the Royal Society in 1660 — the formal beginnings of Natural Philosophy, which today we call (Western) Science. Goethe, Voltaire, and many other philosophers (natural and otherwise) were Freemasons. The writings of many suspected Freemasons mirror the sentiments and arguments found in our lectures, from Sir Frances Bacon to Thomas Paine to Leo Tolstoy. The direction of influence and the degree of coincidence may be argued but is irrelevant. Regardless of the diversity of opinions and intellectual aptitudes among our current members, there no doubt remains a historical connection to such philosophical culture and tradition.

Again, the purpose of this book is to provide a snapshot of this time and place in history. As such, there is as much or more outside the picture as is in it. First, there is the necessarily limited scope of such a very large undertaking. It isn't even known how many groups may fit under the category of Masonic research across the world. There is also the fact that the author worked with limited means and energy.

Also, there is the natural bias of language pervasive in

most fields, that being the English-speaking world versus the rest. I did my best to include Lodges and bodies outside England and the United States. If I have omitted a preponderance of such bodies, it is not through intentional neglect. Given that inconspicuous language bubbles persist everywhere from social media to Wikipedia, I can only surmise how much I may have missed. Further editions, by myself or another, will hopefully present an improvement in this respect.

Some of the information contained herein can be found online. However, a lot of details have been added through interviews and discussions. My intention here is to add a more human narrative behind these groups, fleshing out things you won't find on their websites. Things that might be too personal or contentious (or communicated to me as between faithful breasts) have, of course, been omitted.

Lastly, there is this author's motivation to consider. Masonic research is one of the reasons I joined Freemasonry. If I had not met a Brother of such an interest, I may have not put in a petition at my local Lodge. My goals were few: join Eastern Star with my wife (a lifelong dream of hers); and join the Western New York Lodge of Research. Now I am Patron with my wife as Matron of our Star Chapter (second time), and Worshipful Master at the WNY Lodge of Research (second year). In fact, the research for this book was originally conducted to present the workings of other Lodges as examples of how the author's own Research Lodge could conduct their work.

The content was compiled over a period of two and a half years. Therefore, some of the information may be different than when interviews were conducted and sources referenced. A number of these entities have websites whose domain names have been lost or abandoned, and archived versions has to be accessed. But it is my hope that others may build upon this work for a more comprehensive volume, updated periodically to reflect the state of Masonic Research in future times. For now, the cornerstone, however imperfect, has been laid.

Sincerely & Fraternally,

Bro. Ken JP Stuczynski

* The English word charity is from the Latin caritas, a translation of the Greek word ἀγάπη in 1 Corinthians, which more accurately is translated as Love rather than almsgiving. This is the origin of the three Christian theological virtues, and the three Masonic graces or principle rungs on Jacob's ladder.

Bro. Richard Christian, "Enoch Instructing Hiram Abiff"
(2024) Oil on Canvas, 30″ x 15″

RESEARCH LODGES

Nearly all Research Lodges share a few common characteristics.

First, a Research Lodge focuses on presentations of Masonic topics. Presentations are done at meetings, tyled or un-tyled, by individual members, or sometimes by guest speakers. During the COVID-19 pandemic (2020-2021), many of them switched to virtual presentations, typically on the service which became a household word overnight — Zoom. A rare few did this before the pandemic, but now it is the norm for some of them to at least have them accessible as such and even recorded.

Depending on the particular Lodge, presentations may more likely to be in the form of original research papers rather than contemplative essays or subjects covered like a book report. Standards vary, but most prefer end-note citations. The form desired naturally correlates to the intention or practice of publication. This may be simple email distribution, a (usually yearly) book of Transactions, or even a magazine. Access may be limited to members and subscribers or publicly available. Usually members (and subscribers, which usually include institutions such as other Lodges and libraries) receive some particular benefit, either free digital and/or physical publications or access to otherwise unavailable material.

Secondly, with rare exception, they do not confer Degrees. One must already be affiliated with a Lodge recognized by the jurisdiction in which it operates. Some do not allow Masons outside the jurisdiction to hold an elected office; others do not have such a restriction. Because some consider "Making Masons" the prime directive of a Lodge, some Grand Masters are recalcitrant in granting dispensation, or question the legitimacy of existing Lodges, suggesting they ought to be a club or society instead. Their standing may be specified in the Grand Lodge's Constitutions, and it usually does not count against prohibitions of dual or plural membership.

Like any Lodge, they start with a small number of Brothers seeking more Light. The reaction of the jurisdiction can range from tolerance to enthusiastic insistence to move forward. Grand Masters, sitting and past, are sometimes instrumental in making it happen.

In some jurisdictions there is more than one Research Lodge. They may be regional or have a bent toward a particular historical subject. Statewide Research Lodges may move their Communications or other meetings around the state, going where Temples invite them. Some have their Annual Communication in conjunction with that of their Grand Lodge.

Each Lodge, of course, conforms to the Constitutions and edicts of the Grand Lodge under which it operates. For the purpose of drawing a picture how this works, the author presents the example of the Most Worshipful Grand Lodge, A.F. & A.M. of the Commonwealth of Virginia, which currently has six Research Lodges.

Virginia Research Lodge No.1777 was founded in 1951, followed by five others and one more being planned in Southwest Virginia. Recently, they were placed in a state district specifically for Research Lodges. The other Lodges are are: the **A. Douglas Smith, Jr. Lodge of Research No.1949** in Alexandria, named after the Past Grand Master instrumental in starting it; **George Washington Lodge of Research No.1732**, which focuses on Colonial Era histories; **Civil War Lodge of Research No.1865**, which meets in Richmond, but also at historical locations related to the presentation given; and the **Peyton Randolph Lodge of Research No.1774**, named after President of the Continental Congress and early founder of Virginia's Grand Lodge.

In a presentation of Virginia Research Lodge, the following was given as "the provisions of the Methodical Digest that establish research lodges in Virginia".

> Sec. 2.159. Research Lodges. — A special classification of subordinate Lodges is hereby established, to be known as Research Lodges, with authority to conduct research, hold discussions, gather and preserve Masonic information, maintain a library, supply papers or speakers at the request of other

Lodges when convenient, and conduct a program of general service to the Craft in the field of Masonic education and information, subject to all the provisions of the Virginia Methodical Digest except:

a) The word "Research" shall be included in the name of the Lodge.

b) A Research Lodge shall have no power to confer degrees, and accordingly their by-laws may not specify any fee for the degrees.

c) A Research Lodge shall be exempt from all Grand Lodge dues and assessments, and accordingly shall not be entitled to representation in the Grand Lodge nor have any vote therein.

d) The stated communication of a Research Lodge shall be held according to the provisions of their by-laws. This may result in meetings being held less frequently than monthly.

e) No Brother shall be eligible to be installed Worshipful Master of a Research Lodge unless he shall have already been elected and installed Master of some other Lodge. The provisions of the Methodical Digest dealing with the qualifications of the Worshipful Master shall not apply to the officers of Research Lodges or proposed Research Lodges, provided that before the Master-elect can be installed he must produce a certificate from a member of the Committee on Work certifying to his proficiency in the ritual of Opening and closing a Master Mason's Lodge as well as Calling from Labor to Refreshment and from Refreshment to Labor.

f) Membership in a Research Lodge chartered by the Grand Lodge of Virginia is contingent upon two restricting factors: (1) the Brother must maintain membership in a regular Lodge recognized by the Grand Lodge of Virginia and (2) the Brother can obtain membership only through the process of affiliation. Application for membership must be presented at a stated communication, and if there be no objection may be balloted on at this same communication. At the request of a Brother or at the discretion of the Master, designated applications will be held over to the next stated communication for action. A collective ballot may be taken on all applications approved for consideration at a stated communication. If the ballot not be clear, the Master may have the ballot respread but on this subsequent ballot each application must be balloted on separately. (1992)

g) If a member of a Research Lodge fails to pay the Lodge dues for two or more years, the Lodge may, at a stated communication vote to have the member's name removed from the roll. Such action will not affect that member's standing in a regular Lodge. [See Section 2.158] (2002)

From this, we can see that a Research Lodge is not merely a Square Club or independent society, but a working quarry in the framework of Craft Masonry within the Grand Lodge model. A notable difference, however, is that the Master of a Lodge must have already been the Master of a non-Research Lodge, a stipulation not unique to Virginia. A Research Lodge may also lay outside the district model, or placed in a district specifically for Research Lodges and other outlier entities that may or may not have its own District Deputy. Regardless, these Lodges are regularly Constituted, or under continually renewed Dispensation.

Not every entry in this section may reiterate these common points, and the exact details may be unknown, but attempts have been made to note the unique characteristics and particular differences that make each Lodge distinctly their own.

Quatuor Coronati

United Grand Lodge of England, 1884

Quatuor Coronati Lodge No.2076 obtained a warrant on November 28th, 1884, from the United Grand Lodge of England (UGLE), but was not consecrated until January 12th, 1886, after its first Master, Sir Charles Warren, returned from a diplomatic mission in Southern Africa. It was not formed any differently from any other Lodge except in its focus and aims. After all, there was no previous example to follow, and Lodges in England, as they often do in other jurisdictions, have many themed Lodges, such as those whose members share a profession or particular interest. The introduction of their 133rd Volume of published transactions states

> The founders' objectives were to develop for brethren everywhere an interest in research; to encourage study of the many facets of Freemasonry; to have papers read in the lodge and for them to be opened to discussion and, if appropriate, criticism; to attract the attention and to enlist the co-operation of Masonic scholars in all parts of the world.

With no mandates to do so specifically in their bylaws, they nonetheless presented and published papers and research every year since 1886, along with facsimiles and reprints of rare books and documents in various languages. The founders also established a collection of materials that became a library, currently housed in the Library and Museum of Freemasonry in London, run by the UGLE.

The Lodge's name refers to the "Four Crowned Holy Ones", patron saints of stonemasons for over a thousand years, mentioned in lines 497-534 of the Regius Poem (c.1390).

{Note: *The background story of the formation of this Lodge can be found in the Introduction of this book.*}

Membership

It is not believed to ever have had more than 40 members, similar in size to other English Lodges. It is by invitation only, but due to the high cost of initiation, membership is generally gained only through affiliation. Consideration for membership is based on scholastic experience and ability, with members being expected to be able to independently research and write credibly. Petitioners must be a member in good standing of a Lodge under the UGLE or any Grand Lodge they recognize.

A year's dues are required upon affiliation, regardless of where in the Masonic year, and such is usually done shortly before the start of the upcoming year so as to have this double as a sort of affiliation fee.

The progressive line is generally done by seniority and willingness, and the Master gives a full research paper in the form of his inaugural address. The yearly Prestonian Lecturer, awarded by the Grand Lodge, is often taken from among the members.

Bro. S. Brent Morris is the only Freemason from the United States having served as Master of the Lodge, doing so in 2007-2008. Other members in North America include Arturo de Hoyos, the Grand Archivist and Grand Historian of the Scottish Rite in Washington DC, Mark Tabbert, the Director of the Museum and Library Collections at the George Washington Masonic National Memorial, and E. Oscar Alleyne. The Master to be installed in 2024 (it's 138th Master) is the Grand Historian of the Grand Lodge of British Columbia and Yukon, Trevor McKeown.

Meetings

The Lodge meets five times per year with the full opening and closing ritual, usually at Freemasons' Hall in London. They often meet during Summer months in the provinces and are encouraged to do so to increase access throughout the jurisdiction. Installation is held on the second Thursday in November, to be near the anniversary of the martyrdom of the "Four Crowned Holy Ones" on November 8th, 302 A.D..

Drafts of presentations are sent out ahead of time for review and approval. For all publications, the Oxford Manual of Style is used (an equivalent to the Chicago method in the United States). These transactions, papers, and commentaries, together with book reviews and reports on the content of other Masonic journals, make up the yearly published *Ars Quatuor Coronaturum* (AQC). It is a handsome clothbound hardback, the volumes of which can be found in full at research and reference libraries worldwide, and older volumes can be sold at great prices. Editions have been bound in black for decades, but this year's master noted it was bound in black specifically, "to mark the exceptionally of the past year and the personal losses" that many have experienced.

Publications

To encourage readership and interest, the Quatuor Coronati Correspondence Circle (QCCC) was formed. Open to anyone (including non-Masons), it is managed by regional secretaries in America and Europe, usually from members of the Circle, but not of the Lodge itself. Members, currently numbering around 2400, receive a copy of that year's AQC, and are also available for Lodges or institutions. Outreach includes conferences in the United States, such as in Boston and Alexandria, Virginia, but was suspended due to the COVID-19 pandemic. Looking to expand the conference using virtual tools, they aren't done regularly and often but may become a tradition.

In addition to their website, they have a YouTube channel, and a sister website, 1723Constitutions.Com, celebrating the tercentenary of what is commonly known as Anderson's Constitutions. During the pandemic, presentations and opportunities for questions and answers were done online.

Lodge of Research
No.2429

United Grand Lodge of England, 1892

At meetings of the Leicester Union Lodge of Instruction, Brothers J.T. Thorp and F.W. Billson "formed a scheme to raise issues of Masonic interest" and suggested a warrant be sought for a lodge devoted to research and the dissemination of Masonic knowledge, similar to that of Quatuor Coronati.

Lodge of Research No.2429 in Leicestershire and Rutland was then warranted and consecrated at a Provincial Grand Lodge meeting on October 26th, 1892. Brother G. Speth, Past Master of Quatuor Coronati Lodge, installed Thorp as its first Master. Thorp was "an internationally renowned literary and historical scholar and was the recipient of many fellowships of learned bodies throughout the British Isles" and later became the editor of the Lodge's Transactions.

The Lodge may confer Degrees but chooses not to do

so, so that there "be no trespass on the legitimate areas of the other private lodges, nor the Union Lodge of Instruction". It is also involved with the Hall's Library and Museum. According to its website,

> Over the years the Lodge of Research has become well known over the whole world for its pioneering work in the field of Masonic history. Many Provincial Grand Masters have deemed it an honour to preside over its meetings, and several of the outstanding Masonic scholars of the past hundred years have been included among its members.

Membership

Membership of the lodge is restricted, but Correspondence Circle membership is open to any Master Mason, and have all the same privileges as full members except the right to vote. Normally full members are members of the Correspondence Circle first. Non-UGLE Masons must provide a clearance certificate from their Lodge Secretary.

Meetings

The lodge meets three times a year for lectures and discussions. Correspondence Circle members receive a Summons via email and are invited to attend.

Publications

The annual Transactions booklet has been published

every year since it beginning in 1892. Members also receive a printed copy with an annual subscription of £20 (£25 overseas).

Jubilee Masters Lodge

United Grand Lodge of England, 1897

As per a committee organized at the Especial Communication of Grand Lodge held on June 14th, 1897, and a dinner was held on June 22nd in which only the Masters of London Lodges were invited. The Earl of Euston, Master of Royal Alpha Lodge No.16 and Provincial Grand Master of Northamptonshire and Huntingdonshire, presided. Some of the Brethren present considered forming a new lodge to commemorate the occasion, and 75 of them signed the petition and became founding members of Jubilee Masters Lodge No.2712

In recent years, the Lodge donated over £30,000 to Masonic and Non-Masonic charities.

Membership

Membership is only open to Grand Officers and Installed Masters of or in a London Lodge, but Honorary memberships have been granted over the years.

Meetings

The Lodge meets and dines at Freemasons Hall in London, on the last weekday (excluding Friday) of March and June, and the 3rd Thursday in November. All regular Freemasons may attend as visitors.

Barron Barnett Lodge of Research

United Grand Lodge of Antient Free & Accepted Masons of Queensland, 1903

At the Quarterly Communications of the District Grand Lodge in June 1903, the establishment of a Lodge of Instruction was recommended, similar to the Emulation Lodge of Instruction in London. Its primary purpose would be to improve uniformity of ritual. Consequently, Barron Barnett Lodge of Research No.146 was consecrated by District Grand Master Gregory on August 15th of that year.

It was proposed to name it Adorim Lodge or Dormer Lodge, but instead was named "Barron Barnett Lodge No.3011 English Constitution" after District Deputy Grand Master Barron Barnett, who participated in its consecration and became the Foundation Master. (One source claims the Lodge was to be called "Lodge of Installed Masters, Warrant No.3011".)

Today, members are available to present Lodge lectures anywhere in Southeast Queensland, as well as public presentations on Freemasonry to classes and community groups.

Membership

The requirement for membership used to be that members had to be Installed or Past Masters. Recently though, membership has been opened up to Master Masons.

Meetings

The Lodge meets at the UGLQ Masonic Memorial Temple on the 3rd Wednesdays of January, March, May, July, September, and November, for Installation of Officers. A typical meeting consists of an address, typically by a Lodge member, a discussion topic by member or guest followed by discussion, and a book review by a member.

Publications

Their research papers were published on their website, some being password protected from the profane.

Lodge of Research No.CC

Grand Lodge of Ireland, 1914

The Warrant number 200 was used for several Lodges over the years, dating back to 1749, but most recently applied on March 12th, 1914, to "The Lodge of Research". It was issued "for the association of Installed Masters who are subscribing Members of Lodges under the Irish Constitution, to provide a centre affording encouragement to Brethren interested in Masonic research". The Lodge was formally constituted on September 30th, 1914, by the Grand Master, Lord Donoughmore. It is now known as Lodge of Research No.CC.

Other than performing the Degree of Installed Master on its own newly elected Worshipful Master, it does not perform or exemplify Degrees. It's purpose is "[t]o provide a centre for Freemasons, Researchers and Students of Freemasonry; to encourage and to foster a love of Masonic Research, History, Antiquities and Symbols, by means of the presentation of papers on, and discussions about, such subjects."

{The current status of the Lodge is unclear, as their website appears to have not been updated since 2008.}

Membership

Only those who have served as the Master of a Lodge may become a Full Member, numbered at 232. Only Masons from the jurisdiction may hold an office. Members of other Lodges recognized by the Grand Lodge may become Corresponding Members, members of their Correspondence Circle.

According to their by-laws,

> The Officers and Assistant Officers of the Lodge must be Members of the Committee of Management of the Lodge. In addition, all subscribing Past Masters of the Lodge shall be Members of such Committee. Membership of the Committee of Management shall be subject to annual review. To qualify for Office or for promotion in Office, a Brother shall be a Member of the Committee of Management, and shall have attended at least two of the four Stated Communications of the Lodge in each of the three years previous to his election to any office.

Meetings

A Stated Communication with the installation of Officers is held at Freemasons' Hall in Dublin, in the afternoon of the second Saturday in February. They also meet at Provincial Centres of Northern and Southern Ireland on the 4th Saturday in April, September, and November. Nominations for officers are done in April. All Full Members and Members of the Correspondence Circle may attend.

Publications

Papers presented at their Communications have been collated and printed as softcover Transaction books and booklets since 1914. Many of the earlier publications are out of print, but copies of some are available from stock.

American Lodge of Research

The Grand Lodge of Free & Accepted Masons of New York State, 1931

The American Lodge of Research (The ALR) is "dedicated to researching, documenting and sharing insights concerning Freemasonry using an evidenced-based approach with a goal of inspiring those who are interested in learning more about the oldest fraternity in the world". Founded in 1931, it claims to be the oldest continuous Lodge of research in America. The Lodge was dormant in the years preceding the COVID-19 pandemic but was revived through an initiative of Grand Master Bill Sardone.

Membership

Members of The ALR are made up of Fellows, Active Members, and Corresponding Members from around the world, all eligible to submit research for publication in either *Articles* or "Transactions".

Meetings

Business matters are conducted and presentations for the membership are held quarterly at the Grand Lodge Building in New York City. Occasionally, a Special Communication may be held at another location.

Publications

"Transactions of the American Lodge of Research for Free and Accepted Masons" is printed yearly for Active and Corresponding members, and contain several longer, peer-reviewed articles highlighting their best research that year. Short-form articles are published online for a wide audience to view.

Research Lodge of Oregon

Grand Lodge of Ancient Free & Accepted Masons of Oregon, 1932

Chartered on June 16th, 1932, the Research Lodge of Oregon No.198 is the second oldest Research Lodge in America.

Membership

The Lodge has about 40 members, who may be from any recognized jurisdiction. Officers must be from within its jurisdiction, and many prominent Oregon Masons can be found among its members over the years.

Meetings

The Lodge meets the morning of the 3rd Saturday of the month at the Scottish Rite Center in downtown Portland. The Lodge is typically dark in July and August.

Publications

The Lodge published four volumes of collected papers from 1935-1982, and a book on the Regis manuscript. In recent years, recorded Zoom presentations have been made available. It also has an email newsletter, *Read, Listen, Watch*, available on their website.

Walter F. Meier Lodge of Research

Most Worshipful Grand Lodge of Free & Accepted Masons of Washington State, 1936

Walter F. Meier Lodge of Research No.281 was chartered in 1936 to "serve masonry through research, education, and publications". It also maintains a Masonic Speakers Bureau for presenting research to audiences. It's motto is *Plus Lux* ("More Light").

Membership

The Lodge accepts plural members only, with dues of $60. The exception to plural membership is a number of life members acquired after a consolidation with Maritime Lodge No.239.

Meetings

Stated Meetings are on the 4th Thursday of February, April, June, August, October, and the 3rd Friday of

December. Held at the Greenwood Masonic Center, dinner and fellowship precede the meeting.

Publications

The Lodge publishes content of interest in pamphlet form or in Transactions, including reference papers from other sources. The following are available in PDF form on their website: 2008 & 2009 Transactions; 2010 & 2011 Transactions; 2012 & 2013 Transactions; 2014 Transactions; 2015 Transactions; 2019 Transactions.

Northern California Research Lodge

Grand Lodge of California, 1940

The Northern California Research Lodge (NCRL) was chartered in 1940. Like most Research Lodges, it does not confer Degrees. It's mission is stated on their website as

> [t]o promote personal growth and improve the lives of others. We take responsibility for the well-being of our brothers, our families, and the community as a whole. We value respect, kindness, tolerance, and our differences – religious, ethnic, cultural, generational, and educational, and strive for harmony in our individual lives, in our lodge, and in the global community.

They strive in "Building true fellowship, brotherly love and affection through education, scholarship and research".

Membership

Membership is open to any Mason in good standing.

Meetings

Regular Stated Meetings are held on the 3rd Tuesday of March, May, September and November at the Freemason's Hall of Grand Lodge in San Francisco. They also sponsor special events throughout the year, such as an annual John L. Cooper III Fellowship event.

Publications

Links to the jurisdiction's magazine, *California Freemason*, as well as various articles and videos, are available through their website.

Philosophic Lodge of Research Lodge

Connecticut Ancient Free & Accepted Masons, 1941

Past Grand Master Thomas H. Desmond proposed a Research Lodge to Grand Master Walter H. Pickett, noting that Massachusetts had such Lodges and having one for their own jurisdiction may encourage more to follow. A Petition for Dispensation was requested on May 23rd, 1941, and presented at a special Communication of Grand Lodge at the Bond Hotel in Hartford on October 24th of that year. It was granted as "Philosophic Lodge UD".

The Charter was granted at the annual Communication of Grand Lodge, signed by Grand Master Anson F. Keeler, and presented to the Lodge on February 27th, 1942, becoming Philosophic Lodge of Research Lodge No.400. Past Grand Master Thomas H. Desmond served as its first Worshipful Master, with its first meeting on March 20th, 1942. A 75th Anniversary party was held on March 24th, 2017, with a rededication by Grand Line Officers.

The Philosophic Lodge of Research provides speakers to Lodges and appendant bodies regarding Masonic history, philosophy, and ritual. It serves as the Research Lodge for the Northern half of the state. (The Southern Region is served by the Masonic Lodge of Research No.401, founded in 1966.)

Membership

The Lodge originally proposed a limit of 35 members, with dues of $1. Like most Research Lodges, it does not initiate Freemasons.

Meetings

Programs may be public, for Master Masons only, or ones suitable for Entered Apprentices and Fellowcrafts.

Missouri Lodge of Research

Grand Lodge of Missouri, Ancient Free & Accepted Masons, 1941

Initially voted down by its Grand Lodge, it was chartered under the direction of Most Worshipful Brother Harry S. Truman on September 30th, 1941. It is considered "Iconic within the state of Missouri" and one of the four "Crown Jewels" of the jurisdiction. The Lodge does everything a Lodge does except confer degrees, and "provides brethren with valuable Masonic information and education, quarterly newsletters, an annual book published by the Lodge of Research or a Masonic book of importance, and meetings, lectures, and festive meals".

Missouri Lodge of Research Library

Located at the Grand Lodge of Missouri Masonic Complex in Columbia, the Missouri Lodge of Research Library was dedicated on September 23rd, 2023. Clifton

Truman Daniel, grandson of Harry S. Truman, was a special guest.

In cooperation with the Grand Lodge of Missouri and the Missouri Masonic Research Library, the "Adopt-a-Book Program" was started where individuals or organizations can "adopt-a-book" for $250. These donations are used to digitize their older and more rare holdings, some of which are available on their website.

Denslow Society

The Denslow Society was created as a fundraising effort to "develop and sustain a world class educational resource for the collection, study and preservation of Masonic and Missouri history". A full member who contributes $1000 receives a Membership Patent. Other levels of support offer a lapel pin, neck ribbon, and a copy the book "Denslow Reminiscences". It is the namesake of Ray Denslow, a friend of Truman and possibly the most prolific Masonic author of the 20th Century. Donations support The Missouri Lodge of Research Foundation, a recognized 501(c)(3) charity.

Membership

The Lodge has 500-600 full members. Active Members are Master Masons living in the state, while Corresponding Members can be from other recognized jurisdictions.

Organizations such as libraries and Lodges are considered Subscribing Members.

Members may be designated as Fellows, who must be "a member at least five (5) years in the Missouri Lodge of Research and compiled one or more of the following: Brother has written or published a Masonic subject in a book or leaflet and had general distribution among the craft; Brother has written articles on various Masonic subjects that have been distributed in some publication; Brother has contributed as editor or otherwise to the publication of a Masonic magazine or publication over several years; Brother has completed historic Masonic data and worked on Masonic Research of value that has also contributed in someway to a Masonic Publication or Lodge of Research".

The Master designates a committee to recommend one Brother to be approved by unanimous vote at the Lodge's Annual Communication in September. This has only been done 15 times since 1940, the most recent being Todd E. Creason of Illinois in 2015.

As the Grand Lodge of Missouri is in close amity with their state's Prince Hall Grand Lodge, memberships were given to all Master Masons in their jurisdiction, in the hope of kickstarting their own Research. They receive all publications. The future of this program is in question.

Meetings

Two stated meetings are held yearly and are open to the public, as are the "Truman Lecture" series. One stated meeting is in April or May where a Spring lecture is usually attended by about 60 people. The Annual Meeting at the Annual Communication of Grand Lodge includes a Lodge of Research Breakfast and a world-class speaker, as well as the election and installation of officers. This event consistently sells out, filling whatever the room it is held in. Officers meet monthly, with occasional but infrequent presentations.

Publications

In addition to a blog on their site, the Lodge publishes a quarterly newsletter, containing news, research, informational articles, and items of amusement. The Lodge also sells a selection of books, 70% of which are authored by members.

Virginia Research Lodge No.1777

Ancient Free & Accepted Masons in the Commonwealth of Virginia, 1951

Virginia Research Lodge No.1777 is the oldest Research Lodge in the state, chartered in 1951 with Grand Master James Noah Hillman as its first Worshipful Master. Before modern record-keeping, the Grand Lodge of Virginia would turn to the Virginia Research Lodge to investigate Lodge histories and other questions, such as recognition of Lodges.* It is part of a special district created to administer to Research Lodges.

Membership

Virginia Research Lodge does not Initiate Masons. Membership is nearly a hundred in number, dues being $20 a year with an option for life membership. Any Master Mason in good standing with a recognized Lodge may affiliate and are voted on and admitted on the same day. All members are encouraged to write and present a research paper of their own.

As with any Junior Warden of any Lodge under the Grand Lodge of Virginia, you must receive the Past Master Degree, which is open to any Master Mason. A Warden's Certificate is required to be Master.

Meetings

They meet quarterly in tyled meetings, usually on Saturdays, at Babcock Masonic Temple in Highland Springs, Virginia. A research paper is presented at each meeting on subjects of Masonic history, philosophy, or symbolism, followed by questions and answers. Only Master Masons from a regular Lodge may attend.

Publications

Their Transactions are published in weekly emails, on the web (if appropriate), as well as in booklet form. They also archive papers from other Research Lodges and bodies, including those no longer working. Research papers and information about our upcoming meetings are posted at their Facebook group.

In 2024, fifteen papers have been selected to go into their first book of Transactions, to be titled "Tabernacle, Temple, Self".

* Today, records of recognition are currently available through the Masonic Service Association of North America.

Southern California Research Lodge

Grand Lodge of California, 1952

The Southern California Research Lodge (SCRL), chartered in 1952, is "dedicated to Masonic education and information". It "adopted its service mission of restoring Masonic education and observant practices as a way to expand knowledge of Masonry's history, traditions, symbolism, spiritual and moral teachings and best practices through producing and disseminating written, oral and ritual presentations".

It is best known for its magazine, *Fraternal Review*.

Membership

Only Masons in good standing of a California Lodge can become members. The cost is $150, and the application must he handed in personally at one of the quarterly meetings.

Meetings

The SCRL meets on the 3rd Monday of January, April, July, and October. Since July 2015, meetings have been held at the South Pasadena Masonic Temple.

Publications

Eleven issues of the *Fraternal Review* magazine are published each year for over six decades. Each issues focuses on a specific topic, such as Masonic history, lore, and symbolism. Non-Masons and organizations may subscribe. The SCRL also produces the Fraternal Review Podcast.

Research Lodge of Colorado

The Most Worshipful Grand Lodge of Colorado, Ancient Free & Accepted Masons, 1953

Research Lodge of Colorado (RLC) was founded in 1953 "as a forum of shared insight regarding the rich and compelling history of Freemasonry in Colorado, Freemasonry in general, and to discuss subjects of interest to Masons".

They assert that

> The United States would not exist as a free republic without the influence of Freemasonry integral to its formation. The civilizing force of Freemasonry is perhaps nowhere more exemplified than in the history of the West.

The Lodge met at 1614 Welton Street in Denver for over 50 years, then moved to Highlands Lodge on Federal Boulevard, meeting there from the end of 2019 to February 1st, 2020. It currently meets at Park Hill Masonic Hall.

It uses the motto *Nosce Te Ipsum – Lvx in Tenebris Lucet et Tenebrae eam Non Comprehenderunt* ("Know Thyself – The Light Shines in the Darkness and the Darkness Has Not Overcome It").

Membership

Like most Research Lodges, members must already be affiliated with a Lodge to become a member, and no Degrees are conferred.

Active Members are Master Masons in good standing within their jurisdiction; Associate Members are Master Masons in good standing in an outside jurisdiction in amity with their Grand Lodge. Corresponding Members are Lodges or other Masonic institutions (e.g. Libraries) in the jurisdiction or one recognized in amity. Dues are $33 per year, and all members receive a periodic bulletin, *Lucerna*, published three to four times per year.

Honorary Members are Master Masons, typically Masonic scholars, authors, or others recognized for their contribution to Masonry, particularly in the area of research. Honorary Members do not pay dues but are entitled to all the rights and benefits of membership.

Meetings

The Research Lodge of Colorado meets "at the will and pleasure of the sitting Master" four times a year, on the last Saturday in January, April, July, and October. The current meeting location is Park Hill Masonic Hall in the Park Hill neighborhood of Denver.

Publications

The Research Lodge of Colorado uses The Quarry Project Style Guide for all research papers, and currently plans to publish "Transactions, Research Lodge of Colorado Vol. I. Papers from 1954 to 1960". Its bulletin, *Lucenrna*, is available on its website.

Texas Lodge of Research

Grand Lodge of Texas, 1958

The Texas Lodge of Research (TLR) was set to work under dispensation on December 4th, 1958, chartered by the Grand Lodge of Texas December 3rd, 1959, and constituted February 1st, 1960. It is the only Texas Lodge without a Lodge number on its Charter. Created "for the purpose of promoting, encouraging, conducting and fostering Masonic research and study", they do not confer Degrees, nor do they instate an NPD (non-payment of dues) status for members.

From 1976-1996, TLR also held a "Kenneth D. Gemmell Memorial Breakfast" during the Annual Communication of its Grand Lodge. The presentations at that breakfast are called the "Gemmel Lectures". Since 1977, the "Anson Jones Lecture" has been a request of a recognized Masonic Scholar to give a presentation. Its prestige is comparable to the Prestonain Lectures of the UGLE, and awards the presenter with membership to the TLR. This distinction was given to Brother Oscar Alleyne of New York in 2020.

Membership

Any Master Mason in their jurisdiction or those recognized by the Grand Lodge of Texas may become a member, which entitles them to receive correspondence and publications. Membership is by petition and paying first year's dues of $35. Currently at 650, most Brothers are from the United States, but also as far as England, Australia, Scotland, and Japan. Lodges, Libraries, and non-Masons who receive publications are considered Corresponding Members.

Full Members, who are entitled to hold an elected office, currently number just under a hundred. Leadership is generally a progressive line, based on active attendance. To be elevated to this class, a Brother must present a Lodge history, biography, or other Masonic-related article or paper at one of its meetings. The process for presenting papers is submitting a letter of intent, a thesis statement that must be approved, the submission itself, and then a review. Each year, the Lodge may also elect to admit an additional Full Member with the honorary title "Fellow in Masonic Research" in recognition of their work in the field of Masonic research. The James D. Carter Literary Excellence Award, started in 1986, is given to authors whose presented papers "enhance the image and reputation of the Lodge".

Texas Grand Lodge Laws and the by-laws of the Texas Lodge of Research allow Full Members to wear as their apron a replica of the Republic of Texas lambskin, such as was worn by Sam Houston, Anson Jones, and

other historical figures from the Grand Lodge during the sovereignty of Texas as its own nation. A gold lapel pin of the Lodge is available for Members and associates.

Meetings

A statewide Lodge, they meet four times a year at different locations throughout the state. Events consist of a social on Friday and meeting on Saturday. Widows and wives are invited, and are welcome to join the festive board and any public presentations. During the pandemic, Zoom was used for 2-3 meetings, but it is difficult to find a place with Wi-Fi or reliable Internet connection in some areas of the state.

Publications

The Lodge encourages writing up the histories of Lodges, because of the fear of losing Lodges. They also help Brothers with their research and writing ability.

Their two publications are the *Occasional Bulletin*, often quarterly, and a bound book of Transactions, yearly or every two years.

Anniversary Lodge of Research

Grand Lodge of New Hampshire, Free & Accepted Masons, 1964

Anniversary Lodge of Research No.175 was chartered May 20th, 1964, as part of the 175th anniversary celebration of the founding of its Grand Lodge. For Masons with an interest in Masonic history and philosophy, it "provides an excellent opportunity to see one's work in print, to converse with like-minded Masons and to learn about the activities of other Research Lodges".

They run a "Tri-state Lodges of Research-Day of Light" program, where Research Lodges in Maine, Vermont and New Hampshire meet annually, rotating the event location among them.

Membership

Regular Members may vote and hold office, and must be

Masons from their jurisdiction. Associate Members may be Masons from recognized jurisdictions. Submission of a paper isn't required, but encouraged.

The current membership is 121, plus three Honorary Members, "from all over New Hampshire, from the other New England States from other States and Canadian Provinces, and from England and Australia".

Meetings

The Lodge's Annual Meeting and Installation is held on July 8th at the William Pitt Tavern in Portsmouth's Strawbery Banke. This date marks the anniversary of the founding of the Grand Lodge of New Hampshire.

About four other meetings are held each year, most being visits to other New Hampshire Lodges. Most of these are educational programs, and sometimes a Table Lodge or "Ladies at the Table" event.

They also host virtual educational sessions.

Publications

Anniversary Lodge has published several volumes of its members' papers. It has sent out a newsletter since 2000. All publications are sent to members and a number of Masonic libraries and organizations.

The Lodge also assisted Brother David Crockett of Concord, New Hampshire, in the publication of his book in 1992, "First American Born: The Life and Journal of Jonathan Belcher, the First-Known American-Born Freemason".

Linford Lodge of Research

The United Grand Lodge of New South Wales and the Australian Capital Territory, 1964

In 1963, Sir Edwin Hicks and Robert (Bob) Linford approached their Grand Lodge to establish a Lodge of Research under the name "The Canberra Lodge of Research and Instruction" but the

LINFORD LODGE OF RESEARCH

request was rejected. Grand Master Beers later granted the license that the Lodge operates under today. In 2011, the name was changed to "The Linford Lodge of Research" to honor Bob Linford. His collected works may be available soon through their website.

The Lodge focuses on masonic research and discussion, but in its early years, local Lodges were invited "to participate in ceremonial to be guided and learn".

It joined the Australian Masonic Research Council (which later became the later the Australia and New Zealand Masonic Research Council – ANZMRC) in 1993. Representatives attended every biennial Conference since 1994 and has hosted many of its international touring lecturers.

Membership

The Lodge currently has 12 official members, which must be a Mason from a recognized jurisdiction. There are about 300 corresponding members, which can be non-Masons.

Six of their members have been declared "Kellerman Lecturers", the "most prestigious award for Australasian Masonic researchers".

Meetings

The Lodge meets on the 2nd Wednesday of February, April, May, July, August, October and November at the Canberra Masonic Centre. All Masons may attend and dress is "neat casual with no regalia".

Each Summons provides details of officers and the meeting agenda, with additional information on the topic for discussion. It is accompanied by 'A *Daily Advancement* ...', an article pertinent to the evenings discussion.

Publications

Their website features *Harashim*, ANZMRC's quarterly magazine, as well as other works. They also have an email newsletter.

A previous version of their website had "Transactions of Discovery Lodge of Research No.971", the works of the direct descendant of the Research Lodge of New South Wales and the Sydney Lodge of Research. These contained works from May 2011 forward, consolidated into annual volumes, and were published as an agreement between Linford and Discovery Lodge.

William O. Ware Lodge of Research

Grand Lodge of Kentucky Free & Accepted Masons, 1965

The William O. Ware Lodge of Research is Kentucky's oldest Research Lodge, having received its Charter in 1965. It is named after the Grand Master of the Grand Lodge of Kentucky, 1957-58 who died in 1961 at the age of 52. In tribute to him, Bro. W. Robert Ellis wrote in "The Scottish Craftsman",

> Brother Bill Ware, we believe, had earned every Masonic honor it was possible to achieve. His knowledge of the spiritual and philosophical side of masonry was stupendous. We seriously doubt if any man in Kentucky was possessed of more of the idea of the philosophy of Masonry than was Bill Ware. This editor had the pleasure of seeing him coroneted at Thirty-third degree Mason. And where did he spend his spare time while in Washington? In the library of the Supreme Council. He had a thirst for Masonic knowledge which could not be assuaged.

According to their website, the Lodge "affords an opportunity for Master Masons to enjoy fellowship with each other, while studying and sharing knowledge relating to unique aspects of Freemasonry" and its members engage in "the preparation and presentation of research papers, conduct research projects and publish materials designed to enhance and increase knowledge of the Fraternity" as well as "serve as resources for the exchange of ideas and the facilitation of further research".

Membership

The lodge currently has about 130 members. Officers must be from the jurisdiction and Associate Members may be from any recognized jurisdiction. Honorary Members are chosen based on activity and educational presentations provided to the Lodge.

A designation of Research Fellows started in 2018, awarded to those "[h]onored for creating a lasting body of work over a period of years ... commended for their enduring contributions to the body of Masonic knowledge and for their devotion to the Fraternity and the Craft" and "have demonstrated their worthiness to sustain the legacy of the late Masonic Scholar and our noted Brother, M. W. P. G. M. William O. Ware". The 2018 Class of Research Fellows contained three brothers and one in 2020.

Meetings

Stated Communications are held on 5th Wednesdays, that usually being four times per year, with occasional substitutes to allow for holiday conflicts. The standard location for meeting is at the Temple of Phoenix Lodge No.719 in Walton Kentucky, and are preceded by a meal.

Publications

Voices of Freemasonry is a newsletter of sorts featuring surveys and results regarding Freemasonry. Fourteen papers presented between 1965 and 1990 are available on their website, as well as ones presented on "Papers Night" in recent years.

A series of publications were created as a joint venture between the Lodge and Lexington Lodge No.1. The project, named "Masonic Perspectives: A Second Look at Aspects of Controversial Topics In American Freemasonry", was created by Past Masters John W. Bizzack and Dan M. Kemble, "intended to bring the writings about controversial topics of the past in American Freemasonry and provide readers a second look and contemporary perspective on the topics to serve as a catalyst for further discussion".

The Ohio Lodge of Research

Grand Lodge of Free & Accepted Masons of Ohio, 1966

The idea for The Ohio Lodge of Research started in the 1950s when a handful of Masons started the "Cincinnati Masonic Study Club". It had by-laws but no dues. Limited to 12 members, it required "a paper, typed, double spaced with three copies, on some phase of Masonry as directed by the Club, or some subject of his own selection". The last meeting was held on 1 June 1961, at which time the remaining members (who had dwindled to as few as four per meeting) decided to enlarge the scope of their work by forming a Research Lodge. Its treasured contribution would be a "drawer full of fine Masonic papers of great value".

On 30 January 1965, in Columbus, 64 Brothers were granted dispensation by Grand Master Edgar L. Ott. They received their Charter the following October. The

Lodge "operates for the purpose of encouraging Masonic study and research ... committed to sharing our enthusiasm for Masonry and the Light we have gained through presentations, publication, and fellowship". Together we learn and together we grow.

Norman G. Lincoln Scholarship

The Ohio Lodge of Research provides $1000 scholarships "to assist high school graduates in the endeavor of furthering their education" and "support a general desire for the pursuit of knowledge". Funds may be used for any academically-related expenses at accredited colleges or vocational/technical schools within the United States. Consideration is given to "academic performance, involvement in the community, demonstrated leadership, financial need, and dedication to education". Recipients may apply for renewal in subsequent years with a 3.5 GPA, transcript, and personal letter describing their educational progress. Two such scholarships were given out in 2024.

Membership

Active Members must presented "at least one example of independent Masonic research" to the Lodge, after which they may be nominated and approved for membership at it's annual May meeting. They may belong to any Lodge recognized by the jurisdiction.

Associate Members have full access to electronic resources and can hold an appointed office but cannot vote. They must also be from a Lodge recognized by their jurisdiction.

Annual dues are $12.50, and lifetime memberships are available by paying $50, or four consecutive years of regular dues.

Honorary memberships may be granted at the discretion of the Lodge.

Meetings

The Ohio Lodge of Research is a "traveling Lodge", holding meetings throughout the state at the invitations of local Lodges. Three stated meetings are held, on the third Saturdays in May and September, and the fourth Saturday in January.

Publications

The Lodge's website has virtual archives of various papers, documents, and links to videos, including work outside its own purview.

Masonic Lodge of Research (Connecticut)

Connecticut Ancient Free & Accepted Masons, 1966

The Masonic Lodge of Research Lodge No.401, organized in 1966, encourages work not only regarding the Masonic history in Connecticut, but in "wider and more general topics of Masonic study". (It serves the Southern Region of the state, while the Northern is served by the Philosophic Lodge of Research No.400.)

Membership

Associate or Research Members must be Master Masons, and Subscribing Members may be libraries and institutions.

The honor of James Royal Case Fellowship may be conferred upon "an outstanding Masonic scholar".

Meetings

Lodge meetings are on the 4th Wednesday of February, March, May, September, October, and December, in the New Haven Masonic Temple. Meetings are "typically a short business session followed by an informative speaker, or an original paper by a member, and a discussion circle, possibly with light refreshments". They are open to all Masons, but are sometimes restricted to Master Masons only, depending on subject matter.

Publications

All members receive a digital publication of their Transactions, containing the various papers presented and other "such works as the editorial board may deem appropriate". The Lodge prides itself in having "the first such electronic publication to be issued by any research Lodge".

The Oklahoma Lodge of Research

Grand Lodge of Oklahoma Ancient Free & Accepted Masons, 1966

Grand Master Loflin granted a dispensation to 42 Oklahoma Master Masons to form the Oklahoma Lodge of Research (OKLR) on July 2nd, 1966. Their request stated their desire to "to serve Freemasonry in general, and Oklahoma Masonry in particular, by means of collecting historical data and materials, for the study of any and all phases of Masonic teachings, other than the conferral of degrees, and for other good and beneficial purposes usually associated with Research Lodges".

On February 15th, 1967, a Charter was granted at the Grand Lodge's Annual Communication. At a Special Communication of Grand Lodge on March 11th of that year, the Lodge was constituted and its officers installed by then Past Grand Master Loflin.

Its stated purposes and objectives are

To provide a center and bond of union for Masonic students of Oklahoma.

To attract intelligent Masons to its meetings in order to imbue them with a love for research in Masonic matters pertaining to Oklahoma.

To submit the discoveries or conclusions of students and researchers to the judgement and criticism of their fellows by means of papers read in the Lodge.

To publish special studies for the benefit of the Craft in general and Oklahoma Masons in particular.

To discover, rescue, record and preserve from the loss and oblivion the story of the early Masonic beginnings in Oklahoma.

To assemble a library of publications of general interest to Masonic students and of special interest to Oklahoma Masons.

To establish a museum along the same lines as those indicated for the library.

To collect and correlate material and information for the History of Oklahoma Masonry.

Membership

The Lodge is comprised of 111 Masons and 10 Corresponding Members.

Regular Members from their jurisdiction can vote and hold office, while Masons from recognized jurisdictions can be Associate Members with all rights except voting and holding office. Lodges, Grand Lodges, Masonic Clubs, Masonic Appendant Bodies, or other recognized Masonic groups can be Corresponding Members.

A special designation of "Full Member" is given to those elected as such by a vote of the Lodge for having written and presented a Masonic paper and had it published by the OKLR. Alternatively, it may be considered for "other accomplishments in any field within the purposes for which the OLR is created".

A member may be further distinguished as a "Fellow in Masonic Research" similarly for having written and presented two or more papers or other accomplishments. Only one of these memberships may be given per year, as recognition of distinguished service. James Tracy Tresner II, a member from 1993 until his death, was unanimously elected Fellow of the OKLR.

Meetings

The Lodge meets in January, March, June, and September, at Masonic Temples across Oklahoma, including the Grand Lodge Building.

Publications

Twenty-seven hardcover volumes were published in its 56-year history. Select articles are available on its website, and recorded video presentations appear on the Lodge's YouTube channel.

Georgia Lodge of Research

Grand Lodge of Georgia, Free & Accepted Masons, 1966

Georgia Lodge of Research No.1 was chartered in 1966 to "promote a greater knowledge of Freemasonry among the Craft" by creating opportunities to learn and share knowledge. Several award programs reward those who are to recognized as doing "superior work" in Masonic scholarship.

Membership

Membership is open to all Master Masons of Lodges recognized by their Grand Lodge. Many Grand Masters are among their author-members.

Meetings

Presentations by members and special guest lecturers of "international caliber and renown from inside and outside of Georgia" are given at quarterly meetings and 5th

Fridays. Most meetings are open to guests, and unaccompanied members of the public may attend by special arrangement.

Publications

Their annual hardbound "Transactions" are published and mailed out yearly, containing papers, presentations and essays submitted over the preceding year. They also publish occasional "Bonus Books" and specialty reference tomes, such as "Georgia Freemasons 1861-1865" and "Outstanding Georgia Freemasons".

The imprint on their publications is the "Lit Lamp of Learning".

Florida Lodge of Research

The Most Worshipful Grand Lodge of Free & Accepted Masons of Florida, 1973

The Florida Lodge of Research No.999 was chartered on December 14th, 1973. According to its jurisdiction's prescriptions, "The Grand Master, upon the petition of twenty or more Florida Masons in good standing, may form a Florida Lodge of Research for the purpose of promoting, encouraging, conducting, and fostering Masonic research and study and for the purpose of spreading Masonic light and knowledge and a Charter may be issued to such Lodge of Research without compliance with the usual requirements prescribed for the forming and chartering of regular subordinate Lodges." It celebrated its 50th Anniversary in 2023 with commemorative coins.

Membership

Official members must be in good standing in a Lodge

of any recognized jurisdiction, but officers must be from their jurisdiction. Membership within the jurisdiction does not count as plural membership.

Organizations such as Lodges and libraries can subscribe to publications.

Meetings

The Lodge meets 4-6 times yearly at varying locations, including Grand Lodge.

Publications

The official publication of the Florida Lodge of Research is the magazine *Further Light*.

Illinois Lodge of Research

Most Worshipful Grand Lodge of Ancient Free & Accepted Masons of Illinois, 1976

The first and only Masonic Research Lodge in the state, the Illinois Lodge of Research was chartered on October 9th, 1976, "for the purposes of studying, researching, and recording the history and philosophy of Freemasonry". Like most Research Lodges, it does not confer Degrees. Today, it prides itself "in reporting current events and historical analysis important to both Illinois Freemasonry and Masonry in general" and its meetings provide "a forum for the open discussion of Masonic events, personages, and current events important to Freemasonry".

Illinois Lodge of Research Masonic Education Program is a unique home study program created "to assist the Master Mason in his search for Further Light in

Masonry". Subjects include General Masonic Knowledge, Masonic History, Philosophy, Symbolism, and Esotericism. After various required reading, reports, exams, presentations, and a final project, those completing the program receive the "Pine Cone" jewel of the Illinois Masonic Scholar.

The Lodge also supports the Illinois Masonic Library. Located at the Normal Masonic Temple. Currently is in a period of transition, it is hoped to have regular hours soon with special appointments for members.

Membership

There are currently between 9 and 14 full members, and Masons from any recognized jurisdiction may join. Officers must be from their jurisdiction. There are a few Corresponding Members, and may include "regularly constituted Masonic Lodges, libraries, and related bodies" and receive the Lodge's publications. Annual dues for regular and corresponding members are $10 ($19 for two years) and a lifetime membership is available for $200.

There are 42 Honorary Members.

Meetings

The Lodge holds an annual meeting during Grand Lodge's Annual Communication in October, on the Friday afternoon after the first session. There is always a featured speaker and both members and non-members may attend.

Publications

The Lodge publishes a book of Annual Transactions. *The Lamp*, available on its website, is an online journal for both communication with its members and as a show-case of "outstanding Masonic research and writing". There is also an email newsletter. Video (Zoom) presentations are recorded.

The Heritage Lodge

Grand Lodge Ancient Free & Accepted Masons of Canada in the Province of Ontario, 1977

In 1976, a Regional Masonic Workshop was held in Brantford and Hanover to address the "apparent erosion of ... heritage and apathy towards its preservation" and discuss the idea for a Historical Lodge, followed by a 1977 meeting at the University of Guelph. The culmination of these meetings, some held in homes, was a decision to create an entity in the form of a Craft Lodge.

At a formal ceremony on May 18th of that year, A Petition for a Warrant of Constitution was signed by 104 Charter Members, and Grand Master Robert E. Davies granted Dispensation for Heritage Lodge on September 9th. It was instituted on September 21st under the direction of Waterloo District Deputy Charles F. Grimwood. It was proclaimed and given its number on September 23rd, 1978, with 65 more added as Charter Members.

The two main efforts of Heritage Lodge No.730 are the "presentation of talks and lectures which result in the publication of more than four-score research papers to date" and "special projects implemented to challenge and inspire participants". A more detailed list of objectives on their website reads

> To preserve, maintain and uphold those historical events that formed the foundation of Ancient, Free and Accepted Masonry.
> To Promote the study of Masonry in general, and to provide a service by responding to requests for Masonic information.
> To produce Lodge Proceedings, Research Papers, and Historical Reviews: and to arrange special lectures and visual presentations.
> To organize and maintain a Central Inventory of items of historical interest in the possession of Lodges.
> To encourage participation by Regular Lodges and their members in the activities of this Lodge.
> To endeavour to establish a Masonic Museum.
> To encourage Masonic scholars and Lodge Historians to become more interested in the history of their own Lodges and their artifacts.

A Coat of Arms was regis-
tered with the motto,
"Light from the Past". Its
banner uses the Coat of
Arms with a top caption
identifying the Lodge and
the Grand Register with
the date instituted, and a
caption below indicating
the principle function of
the Lodge as "Research and Education".

The "William James Dunlop Award" is given "to recognize
the outstanding contribution made by a Mason, whether
a member of The Heritage Lodge or not, to the Craft
within Ontario". Given to no more than one person per
year, the recipients' names are added to a plaque for
their recognition.

Black Creek Masonic Lodge

Located North of Toronto, The Village at Black Creek is
a 30-acre of greenspace with "40 heritage buildings, 70
rare and heritage breed animals, and 10 gardens grown
from heirloom seeds". Home to 50,000 artifacts, many
of the buildings are "staffed with costumed educators
who demonstrate 19th Century trades and crafts" and
monthly historical programs.

The Masonic Lodge at The Village at Black Creek is located above the Tinsmith Shop. Staffed with volunteer Masonic Interpreters, its purpose is "to present Masonry in a favourable light to the many visitors who visit the museum each year and to help them understand the place of Freemasonry in the social fabric of an 1867 crossroads rural community".

Membership

Membership is open to all Master Masons in good standing.

Meetings

There are four regular meetings per year: the September meeting is held at the Cambridge Masonic Temple; the Installing Master of the Master-Elect decides the time, date, and location of the November meeting; The March and May meetings are at various host Lodges throughout the jurisdiction.

An annual black tie Heritage Banquet is held on the last Saturday of February or at the discretion of the Worshipful Master. The event features a speaker and the presentation of the William James Dunlop Award.

Publications

The proceedings of Heritage Lodge can be accessed at the Toronto Public Library.

Nevada Lodge of Research

Grand Lodge of Nevada Free & Accepted Masons, 1978

The Nevada Lodge of Research No.2 was founded in 1978 by Grand Master Ovid A. Moore, and is the only Research Lodge in its jurisdiction. They offer a lectures, workshops, and other programs and events throughout the year.

Ovid A. Moore Research Library

The Lodge operates and maintains a Masonic Reference Library and Museum, and is sponsored by all the Lodges of the Southern Nevada Area. It's purpose is to "collect and protect wisdom, works, and memories so that there will always be a great wealth of light.... for those who seek...". It is open to Masons, Eastern Star members, and Masonic youth in good standing. It is located in the East Hall of the Masonic Memorial Temple in Las Vegas.

Opening this year, they are currently accepting Masonic Books, Rituals, and other Masonic regalia for preservation and display.

Membership

The Lodge currently has about 40 members, and officers must be from their jurisdiction. Organizations such as other Lodges and libraries may subscribe to their publications.

They do not have honorary members due to Grand Lodge regulations.

Meetings

Stated meetings are the 3rd Saturday in January, March, May, September, and November, with others as needed. They are held at the Masonic Memorial Temple in Las Vegas. Scheduled meetings "provide a forum where many Masonically related topics may be openly and thoroughly discussed and explored in ways that might not be suitable or proper if done within the body of a regular Lodge meeting".

Publications

In addition to an email newsletter, the first hardbound book of Transactions is to be published in 2024.

Maine Lodge of Research Lodge

Grand Lodge of Maine, Ancient Free & Accepted Masons, 1982

Maine Lodge of Research Lodge No.9000 was organized on April 21st, 1979, and instituted on August 14th, 1981. It received its charter on May 5th, 1982, and was officially Constituted on June 26th, 1982. It is Maine's only Research Lodge, and as such are not part of the Maine Charitable Foundation. They don't vote at Grand Lodge and are not in a district. Their aim is to "enable the Masonic explorer in all of us and satisfy our Masonic curiosity, while learning from each other" and they "deal not only with the historical and philosophical aspects of Masonry, but also with the challenges confronting the Craft". The Lodge also helps connect members with Lodges to provide guest programs. They once did "a public presentation of the Masonic themed opera The Magic Flute that brought together Masonry and the community in a positive and entertaining evening".

The Lodge supports the Grand Lodge of Maine Library through donations, including providing funds for Kindle readers and eBooks. The Lodge itself is unaffiliated with the Maine Masonic College, but members work with them as Regents and teachers.

In 2008, Maine Lodge of Research was the first research lodge in the country to be honored with the Mark Twain Award for Excellence in Masonic Awareness by the Masonic Service Association of North America.

Members

Their 180 members are from across the United States and Canada. Dues are $15 annually or $20 for those out-side the United States and Canada.

Masons whose "contributions to the Craft in their imme-diate communities and for the world at-large" and who "have gone above and beyond and kept the flag waving and standards high for Masonic scholarship" may be rec-ognized as Fellows Of Masonic Research. As per their by-laws, no more than one Fellow is recognized each year, and are not given out every year. Brother Paul Bessel was so honored in 2003.

Meetings

Previously having met quarterly, the Lodge now holds a monthly Stated Communication on 4th Saturdays after a breakfast social hour. After business, a guest presentation or discussion covers "topics of study, discussion, presentation and publishing have included a vast and impressive array of regional, global and historical subjects related to the Craft, directly spawned from the interests our members". Any Master Mason may attend.

The Lodge has also hosted a semi-annual meeting of the Philalethes Society.

Publications

For over twenty years, starting in 1980, the Lodge published an annual book of Transactions, containing their presentations and "other submitted writings of concern to the Craft". The Lodge is planning a new version of the "Maine Lodge of Research Transactions".

In 1984, the Lodge reprinted "A Brief Inquiry into the Origin & Principles of Freemasonry" by Bro. Simon Greenleaf, Esq., a law professor and Christian apologist, and the namesake of an annual award given by the Grand Lodge of Maine.

In recent years, they have been collecting essays by Maine Freemasons on various subjects.

A. Douglas Smith, Jr. Lodge of Research

The Most Worshipful Grand Lodge, Ancient Free and Accepted Masons of the Commonwealth of Virginia, 1983

A. Douglas Smith, Jr. Lodge of Research No.1949, like most other research Lodges, does not perform Degree work. It was formed in 1983 as one of the now six Research Lodges in Virginia. It's motto is "Research Makes a Difference" and has extensive guidelines for submissions as well as provides training in the styles of citations that they require for their research papers, namely Chicago and Turabian.

Membership

Any Mason in good standing of a Lodge recognized by the Grand Lodge of Virginia can apply for affiliation. Dues are $15 per year or $375 for lifetime membership.

Meetings

The Lodge meets on 5th Saturdays at the North Room of the George Washington Masonic National Memorial in

Alexandria. The meetings are preceded by break fast and end with lunch. Attire is tuxedos for officers and "Lodge Shirt, Business Casual or Dark Suit and Tie" for others.

Publications

There are eight volumes of Transactions that cover various years.

Eastern Washington Lodge of Research

The Most Worshipful Grand Lodge of Free & Accepted Masons of Washington, 1983

Eastern Washington Lodge of Research No.310 was established on June 13th, 1983. It does not confer Degrees, and serves the Eastern part of the state. (The Walter F. Meier Lodge of Research serves Seattle and the Western part of the state.)

Membership

Membership is limited to Master Masons, and the number of members is currently 38.

Meetings

The Lodge meets on the 3rd Thursday of January, March, May, July, September, and November at the Spokane Masonic Center.

Western New York Lodge of Research

The Grand Lodge of Free & Accepted Masons of the State of New York, 1983

Near the end of 1981, a small group of interested Masons got together to discuss forming a research and study group in the Buffalo area of New York State. The first informal meeting was held at Buffalo Temple (no longer in use) and subsequent meetings were held in private homes. A notice of invitation to join the group was placed in the local Masonic News, and the Buffalo Consistory offered the use of their Cathedral for meetings and permission to use their library. A petition to form a Study and Research Lodge in Western New York was submitted to Grand Master Bruce Widger on April 12th, 1982. At the Erie County Warden's Seminar, a small group of members met with the new Grand Master, Ernest Leonardi, to discuss their petition.

They received their Dispensation on October 21st, 1982, under the name Western New York Lodge of Research, with Alan G. Fowler as Master. A set of By-Laws were drawn up and petitions for membership were printed for distribution. Several seals were proposed and the chosen design was by Brother David W. Jamison (the image of which was used as an oversized lapel pin years later).

Western New York Lodge of Research No.9007 received their Charter on May 3rd, 1983, making it the second Masonic research Lodge in New York State, and the 68th in the World. They were formally presented their Charter by Ernest Leonardi, Grand Master of Masons in the State of New York, on Friday Evening, March 23rd, 1984.

For years, meetings were held at the Masonic Service Bureau in Amherst, New York. After it closed, meetings were moved to the Cheektowaga Masonic Center, then Sweet Home Temple, and now meet at the Valley of Buffalo's current building in Cheektowaga, New York. For many years, meetings were conducted for administrative housekeeping and informal discussions, but in some years, presentations on specific subjects were the mainstay. Currently, a Trestle Board is set for the following calendar year, and in 2023, the first poster of events was sent to all the Temples in the districts and counties of Western New York.

To better accommodate Brothers in outlying areas, the current Master is attempting to start a tradition where the Master and Wardens are represented by Brothers in each of the three geographic regions, namely Erie

County, Niagara-Orleans, and the Western part of the Southern Tier.

Its current motto is "Demand More Light".

Membership

Membership is open to all Master Masons in Lodges and jurisdictions recognized by the Grand Lodge of New York, and currently has members from around the country. There is no longer a subscriber class of membership, but a mailing list informs those interested, without restriction, of upcoming presentations and the availability of publications.

Meetings

Meetings have traditionally always been held on the mornings of second Saturdays throughout the year, three of which are styled Communications. Today, Communications are held in May (after Grand Lodge) and one other meeting in the Fall. All presentations, unless under special circumstances, can be attended virtually, and are often not restricted to Masons. Some months the meeting may be in the evening of a fifth Tuesday or Wednesday to accommodate varying schedules of members and those interested. Attire is business causal, and the current Master's request is a jacket (tie optional) for Communications.

Publications

A "Book of Transactions" and "Works Under Dispensation" were printed as spiral bound volumes in its early years, republished as a softcover book in 2014. Second and third volumes were published in 2008 and 2013, respectively. A composite volume of all these works, including a paper on the Morgan Affair, was published in 2019, available worldwide in hardcover and eBook.

A repository of recorded video presentations (2023 forward) will be available to members, and a further printed volume is pending publication covering the works from 2014 onward.

Tennessee Lodge of Research

Grand Lodge of Tennessee Free & Accepted Masons, 1983

Formed in 1983, the Tennessee Lodge of Research received its Charter in 1985. It was instituted to assist its Grand Lodge "in its diffusion of masonic light and education by publishing masonic information and educational material" by encouraging Masonic study and research. The motto found on its website is "In Search of More Light…"

Academy of Masonic Knowledge

The Tennessee Lodge of Research's Academy of Masonic Knowledge Certification Process gives members of the Lodge opportunity to earn the designation "Tennessee Master Masonic Scholar". There are three levels with "Masonic Education Units" (MEUs) as a standard measurement for recording achievement. Evaluation Reports are used to determine that a Mason can "demonstrate an ability to identify and apply the Masonic principles" they learn. There is a flexibility in choosing curriculum and participants work at their own pace.

Membership

Any Master Masons in good standing can be members, with yearly dues of $10.

Meetings

The Lodge meets four times a year: on the 1st Saturday of March in the Western part of the state; the 2nd Saturday of June in the mid-state area); the 2nd Saturday of September in Eastern Tennessee; and the 2nd Saturday of December at Sparta Lodge No.99 in Sparta, their "home Lodge". Held at noon, meetings are preceded by a meal and follows with the presentation, which may be from members or non-members. They are usually "non-esoteric in nature so they may be printed in the proceedings" as well as allow non-Masons to attend. Topics include "the history of Masonry (in Tennessee and in general) to the meaning of our symbols, Masonry's place in and contribution to society, Masonic philosophy, and the current state and future of Freemasonry".

Publications

Members receive a mailed quarterly bulletin containing

"highlights and special information" after each meeting, and an annual book of proceedings containing transcripts of the year's presented talks and other information of Masonic interest.

Ted Adams Lodge of Research

Grand Lodge of Kentucky, Free & Accepted Masons, 1983

The Ted Adams Lodge of Research No.998 was Chartered on October 18th, 1983. As a Research Lodge it does not perform Degrees.

Membership

Members can be from any recognized jurisdiction. Their current membership is 126 and includes members from Indiana, Hawaii, Ohio, and West Virginia. Members must be from their jurisdiction to be a sitting officer. There are no subscribing members and honorary membership is prohibited for Research Lodges in Kentucky. Annual dues recently were raised from $5 to $20.

Meetings

The Lodge meets at Chandlersville Lodge on any and all 5th Tuesdays.

Publications

An online repository of presentations and articles is accessible by all Masons within the jurisdiction.

Silas H. Shepherd Lodge of Research

Free & Accepted Masons of Wisconsin, 1984

Silas H. Shepherd Lodge of Research No.1843 was Chartered June 11th, 1984, and is the only duly chartered research lodge in Wisconsin. The lodge's namesake is Silas H. Shepherd, chairman of the Wisconsin Grand Lodge Committee on Masonic Research from 1916 and 1936, and author of many books and poems. He was "nationally recognized for his scholarly writings on Masonic subjects" and elected International Secretary of the Philalethes Society after moving to California in 1934.

Membership

All Master Masons in good standing with regularly constituted Lodges may apply for plural membership, as it does not compete with other Lodges. Masonic libraries and bodies may join as sustaining members.

Meetings

The Lodge is a traveling Lodge and holds their monthly Stated Communication on the 2nd Saturday of March, June, September, and December at various locations throughout the state.

Publications

The Lodge's publication is named "Pharos – The Silas Shepherd Reader" after the Pharos (Lighthouse) of Alexandria, one of the wonders of the world. Ten volumes of "Pharos" are available for purchase in softcover and hardcover, as are the Annual Transactions.

Dwight L. Smith Lodge of Research U.D.

Grand Lodge of Indiana, Free & Accepted Masons, 1985

Dwight L. Smith Lodge of Research U.D., "Indiana's Masonic Educational Resource", operates each year under dispensation and does not confer Degrees. It began almost exactly 167 years after the founding of Grand Lodge, at a banquet held by the Grand Master C.C. "Buddy" Faulkner at the Schofield House, the "birthplace of the Indiana Grand Lodge". He presented paperwork to form a "special purpose lodge with the mission of assisting in the endowing and maintaining of the Schofield House" under the name of Founders Lodge No.1818 Under Dispensation. At the Grand Lodge Communication of 1985, the request was passed. According to Robert R. "Gus" Stevens, who wrote the history of the Lodge found on its website,

> As the years moved on the Founders Lodge 1818 seemed to gravitate to the newly formed Library

and Museum. In 1991, at the annual communication, Grand Master William A. Gallmeister of Evansville recommended that the mission of Founders Lodge 1818 be expanded and allowed to also function as an Indiana Lodge of Research. The Grand Lodge supported this recommendation.

When a new Research Lodge was proposed, one to be called "Dwight L. Smith Lodge of Research", it was decided to have Founders Lodge take on this identity instead. By the recommendation of Grand Master William D. Blasingame, this change was approved. In 1999, it's base of operations was moved from Madison to Franklin. Their current purpose is "furthering research and interest in the history, customs, and societal impact of the Masonic Fraternity" with a mandate "to study these areas from a worldwide perspective, but with a particular emphasis on how they have impacted the lives of Masons, their families, and the general public in the State of Indiana".

Membership

Attendance and participation is open to all Indiana Masons "with an interest in the rich history and heritage of our fraternity in this state" and may join as Full Members. Their by-laws permit Masons from any recognized jurisdiction in Amity with Grand Lodge as non-voting, Associate Members. Annual dues are $5.

Christopher Hodapp, author of Freemasons for Dummies, was Master 2019-2020 and is its current Secretary.

Meetings

The Lodge's two stated meetings are traditionally held after the Annual Communication in May and after Founders Day activities in January. Meetings were abridged during the COVID-19 pandemic.

Louisiana Lodge of Research

Grand Lodge of Louisiana, Free & Accepted Masons, 1989

According to a history written by Brother William Jules Mollere, the question of a Research Lodge was brought up in July of 1982 and for three years there was a discussion "on the merits of developing a forum where Masons could have a point of focus for scholarly talks on philosophy, esoteric doctrine, history, and heritage". Bro. Mollere wrote that he

> had the pleasant task of writing to all of the other Research Lodges in the country requesting information. The Southern California and the Southern Arizona Lodges initially supplied a great deal of information. The Texas Lodge of Research supplied the most helpful material. It was almost as if Texas wanted to repay Louisiana in forming our Research Lodge as Louisiana had helped Texas organize its Masonry. It was a rewarding experience contacting Masonic research organizations throughout the country. All were helpful and encouraging. "Whatever you need" and "How we can help" were the two most frequent replies. Masonry in action – extending that helping hand of assistance.

In 1985, Grand Master Ray W. Burgess appointed a "Committee to Study the Feasibility of Organizing a Lodge of Research". After a few years setting its structure and writing its by-laws, Grand Lodge voted against its formation, but after reconsideration and clarification of cost and consequences, was voted unanimously in favor at Grand Lodge in 1989. Grand Master Eugene Love pushed for its Charter and members were solicited across the state, and in April of that year announced he would be the first to pay dues. At $10 for charter membership, 78 Masons followed suit and on Labor Day in September 1989, the first officers were installed.

No Degrees are conferred. Their motto is "Fostering the study of Freemasonry through Research and Education".

{Please note that according to their website, "The Louisiana Lodge of Research is undergoing significant changes with plans to relaunch in early 2025 with a new website, logo, publication style, and meeting format." }

Members

Today, the Lodge has 32 Active Members, which are made up of Master Masons from Lodges recognized and in amity with their Grand Lodge. Officers must be from their jurisdiction.

There are currently no Corresponding Members, but eligibility includes "Masonic Lodges, other bodies of Masons, Masonic libraries, or any Master Mason who is a member of a regular lodge of a jurisdiction in fraternal relationship with the Grand Lodge of Louisiana". They have no voting rights but receive published proceedings. Dues from corresponding members are slated for the publication account.

Active members can be elected for the honorary title "Fellow in Masonic Research" in virtue of their services and accomplishment related to the Lodge's purpose.

Meetings

Meetings are held bi-annually at various locations.

Publications

Several books have been published, namely the Transactions for each year from 2012-2015, and in 2020 the most recent work was published, a softcover publication of 167 pages. Print-on-demand and eBook versions are being explored.

Research Lodge of the Grand Lodge of Japan

Grand Lodge of Japan, Free & Accepted Masons, 1991

In 1990, Past Grand Master James L. Johnston petitioned to start a Research Lodge under the Grand Lodge of Japan. It was chartered the following year, open to members of all Grand Lodges working in Japan.* Work is done in English only, and meets monthly on a Saturday as a Table Lodge in the cafeteria of the Tokyo Masonic Center. They do 12 toasts, including one to the Emperor.

In 2012, the Grand Master decided there was no need for a Lodge that did not confer Degrees, and so dissolved, or rather caused to continue more as a research society. From this point, there has been very little activity, as members considered it a matter of prestige to belong or even be an officer of the Lodge. The Grand Master at the time of this writing was petitioned to restart it, awaiting a decision.

Membership

Affiliation was as simple as paying a 4000¥ yearly fee (about USD $25). In later years, it restricted its four regular officers to Past Masters in their own jurisdiction (in other words, very few interested Brothers). About 15 Brothers is typical attendance, with not many more paying members, and the majority of the membership is composed of foreign nationals. As with other Lodges in Japan, some Masons use it as an opportunity to practice English, but it seems that more Japanese Masons are of the social persuasion rather than deeper explorations of the Craft.

Publications

Publications are left up to the Master of the year, consisting mostly of monthly papers, often written by the Master himself. However, much of the material isn't published due to the wholesale use of other sources in presentations. Additionally, anything published by Masons on Masonry must be approved by Grand Lodge.

* The Grand Lodge of Japan was founded in 1957, currently serving around 2000 Masons in 17 Lodges across all of Japan. It is bilingual in its work. Many other Grand Lodges had previously established Lodges in Japan, such as the Philipines (on military bases), Scotland, Prince Hall, Massachusets, Shanghai, and the UGLE out of Hong Kong. There is mutual recognition among all these jurisdictions, and they continue to operate under Charters from their respective authorities.

Infinity Lodge of Study and Research

The Grand Lodge of Free & Accepted Masons of the State of New York, 1991

The purpose of Infinity Lodge of Study & Research No.9012 is not actually research, though programs are brought into Lodge now and then. It was Chartered by the Grand Lodge of New York on September 12th, 1991, to allow Lodge life to continue for Masons living as residents of the Masonic Care Community (MCC) in Utica, New York. The Brothers find it stimulating, and effort is made to involve them as they are able.

It was founded by Brother Dennis Breheney, who became its first Master, with the support of the Trustees of the MCC and others. The Master is usually from outside the care community, and for a number of years has been Carl J. Klossner, the District Deputy Grand Master of Oneida District. District Deputies have visited over the years from the local districts (now a single Oneida district), but Infinity Lodge is part of the Special District that includes all Lodges of Research within the state. Grand Master William Sardone presented his address personally there during the three years of his term (2018-2021).

Because of the name and the lemniscate symbol associated with it, sometimes it is referred to as Infinity Lodge No.00.

Membership

Residents of the MCC who are Masons are automatically allowed to join without balloting or dues. These include Brothers who had lived in various places across the state, and their ranks have included Right Worshipful Brothers. Employees and administrators, even MCC Trustees, attend meetings from time to time.

Other Masons affiliate for various reasons ($25 yearly plus a $10 filing fee), such as assisting the Lodge by being officers, there being no progressive line. However, most of the members on the rolls (roughly 35 currently but fewer in times past) are actually Floridians wishing to keep their membership within the jurisdiction. Their yearly fee is $15.

Any Brothers in the state who can no longer easily maintain membership due to their Lodge merging or turning in its Charter such that attending the next nearest Lodge is restrictive due to distance may transfer their membership to Infinity Lodge. This was instituted by Grand Master Williamson (2014-2016) and then an edict by Grand Master Sardone.

Meetings

Meetings are sporadic. They were paused during the COVID-19 pandemic, but have started up again.

Publications

Infinity Lodge does not have any correspondence or publications.

{*During the pandemic, the Lodge was gifted a specially made altar by the author of this book. Ordinarily they had to move a heavy traditional altar from the Administration Building to the "Meditation Room" in the Health Pavilion where they held their meetings. Because of this difficulty, they often used a card table. Upon discovering this during a visit, he set out to build a small, mobile altar with lockable caster wheels, designed to accommodate anyone working at the Altar who may be in a wheelchair, possibly being the first ever intentionally wheelchair-accessible Altar. It features a mosaic pavement on its surface, hooks to hang jewels, and a gold-painted interior for storage of the Bible, candlesticks, cloth, etc.. The underside of the lid features a Blazing Star in Eastern Star colors and an all-seeing eye. The support post contains a time capsule.*}

Temple of Athene Lodge

United Grand Lodge of England, 1994

Temple of Athene Lodge No.9541 was granted a Warrant in December, 1993, sponsored by The Lodge of Harmony, No.255. Consecrated in 1994, it is the oldest lodge in the Province of Middlesex and the Province's Research Lodge. Its purpose is "to study and research Freemasonry and its historical connections, to provide a forum for Masonic debate and discussion, and to stimulate Masonic interest and education principally through the provision of lectures and research papers". It provides lecturers for other lodges within the Province and beyond.

Membership

Applying to join the Correspondence Circle requires completing a registration form and a payment of £12.50.

Meetings

The Lodge meets four times each year for the presentation of a research paper, followed by discussion both in Lodge and over dinner. Minimum Masonic Ritual is employed, and is open to Members, Correspondence

Circle Members, and any Master Mason who is a guest or wishes to visit.

Civil War Lodge of Research

Grand Lodge of Virginia, Ancient Free & Accepted Masons, 1995

Civil War Lodge of Research No.1865 was chartered on November 14th, 1995 at Babcock Lodge No.322 in Highland Springs. Like other Research Lodges in Virginia, it does not confer Degrees. Their research papers share guidelines for submission with the other five Research Lodges in Virginia, being a minimum of five pages and using Chicago Style endnote citations.

Some members commonly dress in Lodge as Confederate and Union soldiers (with swords but not usually rifles). Meetings are often held in "low vales and high places" outdoors, including battlefields. Members participated in "A Gavel at Gettysburg", an event for Freemasons honoring the 150th anniversary of the Battle of Gettysburg. A notable Master of the Lodge was Brother Paul Bessel.

Membership

Members and Officers may be a Master Mason from any jurisdiction, but the Master must be a Past Master and hold a valid warden's certificate from Virginia. There are around 330 members from around the world, including Brothers from Italy, France, and Hong Kong. Dues are $30 per year.

Lodges and individuals can request to be on their mailing list, but this is not considered a corresponding membership.

Honorary members are nominated, investigated, and voted on. These Brothers includes many past Grand Masters from Virginia and other jurisdictions.

Meetings

Stated meetings are held quarterly or more with events throughout the year, held at a location at the pleasure of the Master of that year. In 2018-2019, several Communications were held at Maryland and Delaware Lodges. Zoom presentations were common during the COVID-19 pandemic, and meetings have been virtually available on occasion since. Plans for 2025 include meetings in North Carolina, Alabama, and South Carolina.

Publications

A number of papers are available on their website. A collection of papers are published every 10-15 years, the newest one due shortly and will also be available electronically.

Justice Robert H. Jackson Lodge of Study and Research

The Grand Lodge of Free & Accepted Masons of the State of New York, 1996

Justice Robert H. Jackson Lodge of Study and Research No.9010 was started and developed through the efforts of Brothers in the Jamestown, New York area, such as John Siggins II and its first Master, Stanley Weeks, who brought back news of his travels and visits to Lodges abroad. The name was chosen to honor a famous local Freemason, Robert H. Jackson, an American jurist who served as associate justice of the U.S. Supreme Court, Solicitor General, and Attorney General. Its first meeting was October 29th, 1996.

Membership

The Lodge has between 50 and 60 members, with annual dues of $15. There are no corresponding or honorary members.

Meetings

A few times a year, the Lodge meets at Mount Moriah Lodge in Jamestown, including its annual meeting the 2nd Friday in May. A festive board is held every year for George Washington's birthday.

Publications

Over the years, the Lodge has published four spiral-bound books of Transactions.

Edward J. Wildblood, Jr. Dermont Lodge of Research

Grand Lodge of Vermont, Free & Accepted Masons, 1998

The idea for the creation of a Research Lodge in the state is credited to Grand Historian Eric Ginette in 1994, but not formally planned until April 22nd, 1998, in the offices of Grand Lodge. Brother James Goss, who eventually became its first

Edward J. Wildblood, Jr. Lodge of Research Vermont

Master, and 12 other Brothers, presented a draft of by-laws. Grand Master Edward J. Wildblood, Jr. granted dispensation on August 14th, 1998, with the purpose "to study the History, Philosophy, and Purposes of Freemasonry". The by-laws were approved on the 28th of August and a formal meeting was held September 8th at Granite Lodge No.35 in Barre. At this first meeting, papers were presented and discussed.

Originally named Vermont Lodge of Research No.110, it is the only Lodge of Research in the state. It promotes itself as "an excellent way to both meet new brethren, see the various Vermont Blue Lodges, and receive presentations on interesting masonic topics". Topics may even be non-Masonic "so long as it conforms to our tenets". Not all presentations are meant to be scholarly, but "are a way of educating the members of the Lodge and the Craft at large about Masonry in a fashion which is accessible and enjoyable".

Membership

Any Freemason from a Lodge recognized by their jurisdiction may attend Communications and be members.

Meetings

Business and presentations are done during three meetings a year: at a Southern Vermont Lodge in February; an Annual Meeting at Rutland Masonic Center in April; and at a in Northern Vermont Lodge in September.

Publications

A number of articles were approved to be placed publicly on their website.

Internet Lodge of Research

Grand Lodge of Alberta, 2000

The Internet Lodge of Research was founded in 2000, "at the end of the last millennium", but its origins go back to a group of Calgary Masons in 1993 who wished to form a group called "Internet Masons of Calgary". They found themselves too busy to push the idea forward for a while, but

Internet Lodge of Research
GRA, AF&AM

eventually Grand Master Hugh Young invited Calgary area Masons via email to a meeting to discuss forming an Internet lodge. The first organizational meeting was held on January 28th, 1999, at King George Masonic Temple in Calgary, with 32 Brothers in attendance. After two further meetings, Grand Master Art Jones signed the Dispensation in January of 2000. It was Instituted on March 4th, followed by well-attended Lodge Meetings and workshops.

In 2001, a Charter was requested, and it was decided

to move from two meetings and three workshops to its current schedule of meeting four times per year. The Charter was granted at the Grand Lodge Communication held in Edmonton in June of that year. On the 17th of November, an Especial Communication of Grand Lodge Constituted and Consecrated the Internet Lodge of Research. Grand Master Doug Troock presided and was its first Subscribing Member. The guest speaker was John Belton, Founding Senior Warden and Past Master of Internet Lodge No.9659 EC in East Lancashire, England. It's 16th anniversary commemorative pin, based on its Lodge Seal, features the A.L. date in hexadecimal (greatly earning this author's respect).

The Lodge "is dedicated to research in the area of Freemasonry and technology where the use of the latter can be beneficial to the success of the former".

Membership

At this time, full membership is restricted to Master Masons from their jurisdiction, though there have been officers from around the world in the past.

Subscribing Membership is open to any Mason from a recognized jurisdiction in amity with The Grand Lodge of Alberta. They may submit research, and have access to the member area of their website. As a requirement, they must maintain a valid email address. Subscribing involves an application with a one-time fee of CDN$25.

Only Past Masters who are full members may be elected as Master or Warden.

All members and visitors receive their anniversary commemorative pin.

Meetings

The Lodge currently meets at Bowmont Masonic Hall in Calgary in the morning of the 3rd Saturday of February, September, and November, and the 1st Saturday of June. Attire is business casual, and Masonic guests are welcome.

Meetings feature primary and secondary presentations (the latter of which which may be virtual), sharing of Masonic and technical experiences by Brothers on the Internet, and time to ask technical questions of learned Brethren.

Pennsylvania Lodge of Research

Grand Lodge of Free & Accepted Masons of Pennsylvania, 2000

Arising from a "turn-of-the-century renewed interest in Masonic education in Pennsylvania", the Pennsylvania Lodge of Research No.1 became the first Lodge in the state constituted "solely for the purpose of Masonic study". Grand Master Robert L. Dluge warranted it on December 27th, 2000. This "culmination of a concept espoused for many years by Thomas W. Jackson, Right Worshipful Past Grand Secretary" took form in discussions by the Grand Lodge Masonic Culture Committee. Applications to become founding members were taken through the Masonic Education Committee, and numbered almost 200 by the end of 2001.

Degrees are not conferred, the Worshipful Master does not receive "the Word of the Chair", does not wear a top hat, and is not a voting member of Grand Lodge. Floor Officers wear tuxedos but do not wear gloves. Officers have special aprons with a distinctive burnt orange color authorized for use of the Lodge when in session. Members wear a Member's Jewel in the suit coat breast pocket, with Charter members having a white stripe on their ribbon. It cannot be worn at other Lodge meetings.

The Pennsylvania Lodge of Research has it's own medallion, described thusly:

> [It] depicts a classical female allegorical figure holding a manuscript in one hand and a square and compasses in the other. The sunburst represents Enlightenment. Its symbolism is obvious in depicting the purposes of the Lodge of Research as sharing Masonic Light with others who are following a planned approach to personal character-building and self improvement, and to encourage an organized process of formal education of the Craft at large.

It aims to provide "exposure to new ideas through meetings and published transactions, as well as information about unique and rare documents and publications".

Members

Full membership is extended to Masons within the jurisdiction, and does not constitute dual membership. Associate membership is extended to Brethren of other jurisdictions recognized by their Grand Lodge. Dues are $25 per year with a $75 petition fee. Members receive a Member's Pocket Jewel and a Lapel Pin, and are entitled to received the published Transactions.

Following the example of Quatuor Coronati, a research paper is delivered by the Worshipful Master upon his installation, which is in December.

Fellows may be elected to be honored as distinguished members for their outstanding scholarship.

Meetings

Two Stated Meetings are held each year, with Special Meetings held at the Worshipful Master's discretion. Locations vary across the state. Masonic topics include those that "further our understanding of our Fraternity, including its history, philosophy, and symbolism". Any member of a Lodge recognized by and in amity with their jurisdiction may attend.

Publications

The Lodge published eight volumes of Transactions thus far. In 2015, the Quarry Project was adopted as its research style guide.

New Jersey Lodge of Masonic Research and Education

The Grand Lodge of New Jersey Free & Accepted Masons, 2001

The New Jersey Lodge of Masonic Research & Education, No.1786 was constituted by Grand Master David A. Chase in 2001, the number given being the year of the formation of its Grand Lodge.

Its purpose is "to foster the education of the Craft at large through prepared research and open discussion of topics concerning Masonic history, symbolism, philosophy, and current events". According to its website, it offers its members Fraternity, Scholarship, and Prestige, where like-minded Masons have the opportunity to share research that adds to the body of Masonic knowledge.

Submission criteria for papers to be presented include subject matter being related to Freemasonry and end notes.

Membership

Freemasons from all parts of the state of New Jersey make up the Lodge's membership, and any Mason from a Lodge recognized by their jurisdiction may join. The yearly dies are $25 with a petition fee of $25.

Laureate Members are those who prepare and present five papers for publication, and members earn the title of Distinguished Laureate by presenting ten papers. Distinguished Laureate Emeritus is a title that may be conferred by the Master with the approval of the Lodge "upon a brother with considerable merit".

Meetings

The Lodge meets on the 2nd Saturday of March, June, September, and December and is open to all Master Masons.

Publications

A quarterly bulletin is mailed to members, containing "highlights and special information after each meeting".

Each year the Lodge publishes all of the papers prepared and submitted the previous year. This publication is known as the "Transactions of the NJ Lodge of Masonic Research and Education No.1786".

James M. Simms Lodge of Masonic Research

Most Worshipful Prince Hall Grand Lodge of Georgia, 2002

This Prince Hall Lodge of Research was named after Rev. James M. Simms, the founder and first Grand Master of Prince Hall Freemasonry in the State of Georgia. Born a slave, he was a carpenter by trade, and having been taught literacy illegally, was "the only black person known to be punished in Savannah for teaching blacks to read and write". During the Civil War he went to Trinidad and then to Boston, and joined the Union army. After the war, he was appointed as a Judge on the Chatham County District Court but due to racist controversy, he went back to being a customs official. When the "The Georgia Industrial College for Colored Youth" was established, he became it first proctor. A monument was placed over his grave in June 1920 by The Most Worshipful Prince Hall Grand Lodge of Georgia.

The Lodge itself began at Grand Lodge Session in June 2002 with Brother Joe H. Snow presenting the idea to Grand Master William L. Williams, who "would support it totally, and the rest is history". According to its website,

This is something that is long over due for Prince

Hall Masonry. There has not been a Research Lodge for Prince Hall Masonry since the first and only Research Lodge that came under the jurisdiction of the Most Worshipful Prince Hall Grand Lodge of New York titled "PHLORONY" Prince Hall Lodge of Research of New York, which was started in 1943 under the stewardship of R. W. Harry Williamson Past Deputy Grand Master.

The Lodge is "committed to promoting Masonic Research and Education by providing a forum for presentations of papers on Masonic subject and publication of a Quarterly Masonic Journal".

{This book contains information on one other Prince Hall Lodge of Research under "Other Lodges"}

Membership

Any Mason under their Grand Lodge may apply to become a Member. Anyone else may become a Corresponding Member.

Publications

The Lodge has committed to publishing a quarterly Masonic journal.

Forskningslogen Niels Treschow

Den Norske Frimurerorden (Order of Norwegian Freemasons), 2003

Forskningslogen Niels Treschow (Niels Treschow Lodge of Research) is named after Niels Treschow (1751-1833), a prominent Norwegian Freemason, philosopher, scholar, and politician. It is organized under Order's Banner Bearer (OBF), which heads the Knowledge Directorate (KD).

Constituted November 1st, 2003, at the Order's headquarters, it was decided by The Supreme Council (DHR) on April 4th earlier that year that a nationwide research Lodge be established.

Its purpose is for research on "the content of Freemasonry, its historical and cultural background and development, its social significance and ideological basis". It can be on any Masonic topic but focus on "Masonic systems that are used, and have been used, in Norway". It shall "promote such research among the brothers and disseminate the results of this research among its members and the Order's other brothers". According to their website,

> [t]he research lodge has small and large projects, but usually requires research in domestic and foreign archives and a review of primary and secondary literature. The project must be approved by the FNT management in advance, but then it is usually just a matter of starting the work. Everything that is researched is communicated to the brothers orally via a lecture in a lodge or in writing through an article in Acta or Verba {see below}.

Its proposed coat of arms and badge has the motto "*Per scientiam ad certitudinem*", meaning "Through knowledge to certainty".

Membership

Membership consists of 27 members, appointed by the Grand Master of the Order (OSM) for four years at a time. Officers are appointed from the membership and must be from their jurisdiction.

There are about 1400 corresponding members, which must be Master Masons (III Degree and above) in a Lodge recognized by their jurisdiction.

Meetings

Four or more meetings are held each year, most at the Orient in Oslo and at least one at a Lodge elsewhere in Norway. Six meetings were held in 2023. At each meeting, a member presents their research and materials.

Publications

"Acta Masonica Scandinavica" (Acta) is a hardcover book published annually, typically 200 to 300 pages. It normally contains seven to ten research papers from this and other Scandinavian Lodges (Friedrich Münter in Denmark, Carl Friedrich Eckleff in Sweden, and Snorri in Iceland).

Verba is the Lodge's printed 8-page newsletter / magazine distributed four times each year. Some content gets republished in the *Frimurerbladet* (Masonic Magazine) and "Acta". Content by members outside the permanent 27 may be submitted for inclusion.

An email newsletter is sent to all members before meetings. There are also recorded video presentations.

Massachusetts Lodge of Research

The Most Worshipful Grand Lodge of Ancient Free and Accepted Masons of the Commonwealth of Massachusetts, 2008

The Massachusetts Lodge of Research was formed in 2008 with a strict focus on historical research. However, "being created right on the cusp of mass digitization of records, and exciting new advances in technology for both research and organizational purposes", its work opened to broader "well developed and carefully sourced knowledge" useful to Freemasonry. Today, it continues its mission "to spread light and expose brethren to history, philosophy, practices, technology and any other topic that pertains to the past, present and future of the Craft".

Membership

Dues are $20.88 per year.

Meetings

Quarterly meetings are on Saturday mornings in February, May, August, and November. They are held in various parts of the state and often accessible online.

Mississippi Lodge of Research and Education

The Grand Lodge of Mississippi Free & Accepted Masons, 2009

Mississippi Lodge of Research and Education DCXL (No.640) was granted dispensation by Grand Master William R. Robinson on August 27th, 2009. The principal officers were the three Master Masons who first approached him about instituting such a Lodge: Christopher M. Reid of John P. Byrd No.629 in Pearl, Mississippi; Edgar A. Gonzales-Loo of Jose Galvez Egusquiza No.75 in Ilo, Peru; and James S. Goode of Bolton No.326 in Bolton, Mississippi. Until being granted a Charter at Grand Lodge's Annual Communication on February 9th, 2010, they met at the Hall of Pearl Lodge No.23, located on the third floor of City Hall in Jackson, Mississippi.

Its mission statement is to "provide opportunities, guidance and direction in development of Masonic education, research and assist in defining practical applications, based upon; past, present and future best practices to the betterment of Mississippi Freemasonry by recognizing and supporting the history, traditions, symbolism, spiritual and moral teachings of the Grand Lodge of Mississippi and promoting best practices through producing and disseminating written, oral and ritual presentations". Their events include training and education on Lodge management, such as the work of an investigation committee.

Collegium Masonicum

The Mississippi Lodge of Research and Education DCXL operates the "Collegium Masonicum" (Masonic College). Its purpose is to "serve as the voice of all Lodges under the jurisdiction of the Grand Lodge of Mississippi regarding research activities and to provide a Curia to exchange ideas, promote harmony and fellowship and to increase overall awareness of Mississippi's Masonic history". It is composed of delegates, one from each of the Lodges who have a member in the Research Lodge. The presiding "Master of the Masonic College" is the Master of the Research Lodge and makes all appointments. In 2023, there were delegates from 21 Lodges.

Membership

The Lodge has 52 members at the time of this inquiry. They are all dual or plural members except in special circumstances as prescribed by the Grand Lodge. Official members may be from any recognized jurisdiction.

Those who have "demonstrated outstanding scholarship in Masonry and service to the Mississippi Lodge of Research DCXL" are given the distinction of Fellow and are entitled to use the honorific "FMR" after their name. Only two Brothers have been given this distinction thus far, Past Masters Christopher M. Reid in 2010 and W. Terry McLeod in 2019.

Meetings

Grand Lodge amended its Statutes to permit the Lodge to have quarterly Stated Communications and to meet anywhere within the jurisdiction. Stated Communications are held four times a year "according to the schedule of the full moon" at the Hall of the Masonic York Rite of Jackson. They manner themselves an "Observant Style Lodge" with the use of music, incense, and period of contemplative silence, concluding with a solemn "Chain of Union". Meetings are primarily in Jackson, but travel to other Mississippi Lodges. Attire as per their custom and bylaws is a suit and tie.

Presentations may be during the meal, in the Lodge

room, or in a non-tiled session. Papers can be "of a strictly historical or biographical nature [that] are rarely entertained in the Lodge room", or regarding symbolism, initiation, ritual, metaphysics, philosophy, and art. Other topics may relate to Freemasonry "within the context of the major world religions, esoteric movements such as Gnosticism, Hermeticism, Neoplatonism, Rosicrucianism, Kabbalah and many other Western and Eastern traditions".

Publications

Numerous whitepapers have been published on best practices for archival techniques and preservation policies. These papers range in subjects from furniture and natural history specimens to disaster response and recovery.

Alabama Lodge of Research

The Most Worshipful Grand Lodge of Free & Accepted Masons of the State of Alabama, 2010

Grand Master Larry A. Hancock issued a Warrant to establish the Alabama Lodge of Research (ALOR) on August 30th, 2010. On November 9th, it met for the first time and became its Annual Communication. It was held at the Scottish Rite Masonic Center in Montgomery.

Its mission is "to provide the Freemasons of Alabama a source for knowledge and education about the history of Freemasons and Freemasonry within the State of Alabama" and "act as a repository for papers, videos, and other media, of historical significance in an online format".

Membership

Membership is available to all Master Masons in good standing from a Lodge under the jurisdiction of a Grand Lodge of North America. Regular members are those within the jurisdiction; Associate members are those outside the jurisdiction and have all the rights and privileges except voting or holding office.

All memberships provide access to all digital archives. The petition fee is $30 with $20 due annually.

Publications

Their website, under reconstruction at the time of this being written, at one time had historical information, a digital version of the Proceedings of Grand Lodge, informational videos, and a member-only discussion forum. They have been working to compile Alabama Lodges histories as well.

George Washington Lodge of Research

Ancient Free & Accepted Masons in the Commonwealth of Virginia, 2012

The idea for George Washington Lodge of Research No.1732 came from an exemplified Colonial American Entered Apprentice Degree at the Peyton Randolph Lodge of Research No.1774. This Degree was held at Reid James Simmons Academy of Masonic Leadership in 2009. In their words:

IN LUCE SCIENTIAE REPERIRI POTEST FIDES,
CONFIDO ET SAPIENTIA.

> [Brother Shelby] Chandler realized that the ritual was based upon English Freemasonry. Being a member of Fredericksburg Lodge No. 4, he was aware that his Masonic Lodge not only had a long Scottish heritage, but it also had a rich history by which much could be recovered. While reviewing that history, he realized the probability that colonial ritual work in America could be different according to the Grand Lodge to which a colonial Lodge was beholden to in that period. Brother Chandler discussed this realization with Worshipful Jene G. Parrotte and Worshipful Jeffrey D. St.

Onge and eventually other Virginia Masons joined in with the discussions, so it was decided to identify this new Lodge with a historic Virginia Mason to give it focus.

At the 2011 National Convention of the National Sojourners in Richmond, signatures were garnered for this purpose. Most Worshipful William Talbott Ellison, Jr. issued a dispensation on August 4th, 2012, and it was chartered during the Grand Annual Communication on November 7th, 2012. Shelby L. Chandler, II became its first Worshipful Master.

In so naming the Lodge they "acknowledge that Illustrious Brother George Washington was more than just a good man and Freemason ... not just as a National figure, but as an International Masonic icon". He is quoted on their site, "Knowledge is in every country the surest basis of public happiness."

Their stated purpose is "to bring brethren together for ... both Masonic and Academic enlightenment; to recover the fragmented heritage of our historic past and to chronicle and document these moments in time for posterity".

Membership

Members may be from any recognized jurisdiction, and presently number around 60. Organizations can subscribe to publications.

Meetings

Meetings are held quarterly at Fredericksburg Masonic Lodge, the Mother Lodge of Brother George Washington.

Publications

Research papers are published publicly on their website. Also available are presentations by charter member Brother Bob R. Melvin, Jr., the Lodge Education Officer of Fredericksburg Masonic Lodge No.4.

COLLEGIVM LVMINOSVM Lodge of Research

Grand Lodge of Freemasons of Rhode Island A.F.&A.M., 2015

COLLEGIVM LVMINOSVM Lodge of Research, the "Masonic College of Light in Rhode Island", was chartered on March 30th, 2015. Because they do not confer degrees, they do not consider themselves a Symbolic Lodge and therefore decided not to have a number.

They use titles inspired by Oxford tradition, such as Chancellor, Vice Chancellor Pro-Vice Chancellor, and a Bedel with a mace, similar to a Marshal. The executive board is called a Regent House. The dress code is "Shaw's academic attire", open robe style with a subfusc under robe (like black tie attire with white tie). They use Christian calendar terminology but are not closed to other faiths.

Membership

The Lodge has about 50 members. Officers must be from their jurisdiction. Scholars (general members) can be voted to become a Fellow if they present a paper.

Meetings

In addition to an Annual Communication, the hold three other Communications during the year at various Lodges and the Scottish Rite Valley. Meetings were held via video presence during the COVID-19 pandemic, but are currently not virtual nor recorded.

Publications

They do not currently have enough papers to publish a book, but many are published elsewhere. Older newsletters can be found on their website.

Lebanon Research Lodge

Grand Lodge F.&A.M. of Lebanon, 2018

On October 24th, 2018, a new Charter was granted by the Grand Lodge of the State of New York to form the Grand Lodge Free & Accepted Masons of Lebanon, composed of many of the Lodges from the former's District of Syria-Lebanon. From this new body, nine members of the "Toward the Sunrise" Masonic club applied for and received a Charter on November 26th, 2021 for the Lebanon Research Lodge (LRL).

They have two mottos: "*Quo Lux Lucet*" ("Toward the Sunrise", alluding to Joshua 13:5); and "The Equality of all, and the Liberty of each", a quote from a Phoenician, Papinan the Jurist (179 AD).

Membership

Currently, membership is only its nine founders, but petitions for affiliation are already being examined, as it will be open to all Master Masons in their jurisdiction. Brothers from other recognized jurisdictions will be allowed as Associate (non-voting) Members, and up to two Honorary Memberships can be given out each year for contributions to Masonic scholarship. There are only four main officers (Master, Secretary, Treasurer, and Chaplain), and no Degrees are conferred. As per the

Grand Master's decree, per capita fees have been suspended across the jurisdiction, and the Lodge will not be collecting fees at this time due to current economic hardships.

Meetings

They meet quarterly, either in person or online. When in-person, they meet in conjunction with one of the Lodges in the Jurisdiction, often being opened and closed by the Lodge visited. A short special ritual was created and is used for opening and closing that is appropriate for video conferencing. It consists of asking the Blessings of the GAOTU on the work and members present. The work is done primarily in English and if needed, Arabic and French.

Any research topic of value to Masonry or Lebanon can be discussed, but the Master is charged to provide at least one topic specifically related to Lebanon.

Publications

Their plan is to publish its presentations digitally each June (as a PDF), and have its members available to share their research with any Lodges, in or recognized by, the Grand Lodge of Lebanon.

Other Research Lodges

{*Due to time constraints, the author was unable to include all the Lodges found mentioned in various listings online. For some Lodges, there was little or no information online and no way known to him to directly contact them. Therefore, the following are listed to cursorily mention those Lodges which are believed to currently exist in recent years. As the date of their creation is unknown for many of these, they are arranged geographically and by number or name.*

It is the author's hope that with help, and possibly hearing from these Lodges after the publication of this edition, more comprehensive entries may be made.}

United Kingdom

United Grand Lodge of England

Sussex Masters' Lodge No.3672
In Brighton

East Sussex Masters' Lodge No.8449
In Battle

Bishop Surtees No.8497
Meets in Topsham, Devon; Consecrated in 1973

West Sussex Masters' Lodge No.8963
In Chichester

Worthing Installed Masters' Lodge No.9860
Consecrated in 1980; meets in Chichester

Seven Sisters Installed Masters' Lodge No.9918

The Richard Sandbach Lodge of Research No.9600
In Peterborough

Veritatem Sequere Lodge No.9615
Consecrated May 24th, 1996; meets in St. Albans 1st Friday in October for Installation, 4th Monday in January, and 2nd Wednesday in July

Grand Lodge of Scotland

The Lodge, Hope of Kurrachee No.337
Provincial Grand Lodge of Fife and Kinross; meets at Rosyth on the 3rd Friday of February, September and November, with installation on the 3rd Friday in April

Felix No.355
Located in Peterculter, Province of Aberdeen West; meets the 3rd Saturday of April, June, and November in the afternoon

Lodge Sir Robert Moray, No.1641
Primarily a Research Lodge, it dates back to February 1st, 1968, and meets on the same day as the Grand Lodge Communications in Edinburgh; named for Sir

Robert Moray, initiated by the Lodge of Edinburgh in 1641 — the first record of a non-operative being admitted on English soil

The Anchor Lodge of Research No.1814
Located in Greenock, Province of Renfrewshire West; Meets on the 1st Friday of April, May, September, and October in the afternoon

United States

Most Worshipful Grand Lodge of Free & Accepted Masons of the State of Alabama

Confederate Military Lodge of Research
Created by Warrant August 6th, 1990; members must be from a recognized Lodge and have "a documented lineal or collateral ancestor who was a Confederate Veteran or member of the Confederate Government"; dues are $20 with a lifetime membership option for $100; monthly email newsletter "Southern Light" {may be defunct}

Grand Lodge of Free & Accepted Masons of California

El Camino Research Lodge
Monthly Stated meetings are on the fourth Friday of every other month

Golden Compasses Research Lodge
Meets four times a year in Folsom

Orange County Research Lodge
Open to all Master Masons; meets on 3rd Wednesdays of February, May, August, and November at Gateway Lodge in Brea

Most Worshipful Prince Hall Grand Lodge, District of Columbia

David A. McWilliams, Sr. Research and Education Lodge
This unique Lodge is "dedicated to the conduct of research and education about Freemasonry in general and Prince Hall Freemasonry, in particular, so it can illumine the Masonic Fraternity and be better agents of change and service in their communities". Its first Worshipful Master was Alton Roundtree, former Editor of the jurisdiction's Masonic Digest.

District of Columbia

Pythagoras Lodge of Research and Museum (in Washington, D.C.)
Not a Lodge in the usual sense, it was established July 16th, 1890 to oversee the Museum's collection of art from ancient Egypt. Its archives are "comprised of over 6500 linear feet of museum records, manuscripts, personal papers, ephemera, scrapbooks, photographs, videotapes, films, and artifacts that chronicle the history

of Freemasonry" and has "approximately twenty-six thousand objects of artistic, historical, and cultural importance, dating from the Paleolithic to the Roman period". It also has "papers from individuals related to Freemasonry, documents from family and other members; records of affiliated organizations such as the Knights Templar and The Grottos; and other primary research materials related to the museums properties and art collections".

The Most Worshipful Grand Lodge of Ancient Free & Accepted Masons of Delaware

Delaware Lodge of Research
Located in Wilmington

Grand Lodge of Georgia, Free & Accepted Masons

Research Lodge No.1
Located in Savannah

Lodge of Research No.10 of North Georgia
Meets 2nd Saturdays in January, March, May, July, September, and November; has different levels of membership based on access and responsibility

Grand Lodge of Iowa, Ancient Free & Accepted Masons

The Iowa Research Lodge No.2
Meets 1st Tuesdays

Grand Lodge of Kansas Ancient Free & Accepted Masons

Kansas Lodge or Research (KSLOR)
Styling itself "The Future of Masonic Research", it has five divisions — Archival, Virtual, Esoterics (reading lists, newsletters, etc.), Speakers, and Publishing.

Grand Lodge of Kentucky, Free & Accepted Masons

Marlin White Lodge of Research
Chartered in October of 2018; meets in Cave City; named in honor of Grand Master Marlin White (1982-1983)

The Grand Lodge of Maryland

Maryland Masonic Lodge of Research No.239

Grand Lodge of Michigan, Free & Accepted Masons

The Michigan Lodge of Research & Information No.1
Chartered 29 May 1985, it is located on on the 5th floor

of the Detroit Masonic Temple. It is the successor of the Masonic Library of Detroit (1882-1932). On 26 January 2019, for the first time ever, a Prince Hall Mason, Harry Weaver, presided over a Lodge within their jurisdiction. May be defunct.

Alexandria Lodge of Research and Study Lodge No.2
Meets quarterly at the Grand Rapids Masonic Center; open to all recognized Master Masons; promotes the Michigan Masonic Museum & Library

Pythagoras Lodge of Research & Information No.3
Based in Lansing; meets four times a year; organized August 15th, 2017 by 20 Brothers from nine area Lodges; active and current members of a Blue Lodge in Michigan may join

Fiat Lux Lodge of Research & Education No.4
In Marquette

The Grand Lodge of Ancient Free & Accepted Masons of New Mexico

Lodge of Research of New Mexico
Meets at least four times per year in various locations and encourages the forming of related clubs; publishes the *La Luz* newsletter quarterly

The Grand Lodge of Virginia

Peyton Randolph Research No.1774 (The Grand Lodge of

Virginia)
Meets 4th Saturdays in January, April, July, and October, in Colonial Williamsburg; focuses on Colonial Freemasonry and the founding of its Grand Lodge

James Noah Hillman Lodge of Research No.1883
Chartered in 2009; met in Southwest Virginia — no longer active

The Most Worshipful Grand Lodge of Free & Accepted Masons of Washington

Walter F. Meyer Lodge of Research No. 281
Meets in Seattle on 4th Thursdays in February, April, June, August , October, and the. 3rd Friday in December

Canada

Grand Lodge of Alberta

Fiat Lux No.1980

Grand Lodge of British Columbia and Yukon

Vancouver Lodge of Education and Research
Six meetings per year in the Vancouver Lower Mainland area; sponsors the annual Vancouver Grand Masonic Day

Victoria Lodge of Education and Research
Meets at the Masonic Hall in Victoria on the 3rd Tuesdays of February, March, April, September, October, and November ("MASON"); not Chartered, but "operates under special license from the Grand Master which is renewed every year".

South America

Grand Lodge of Chile

Lodge of Research Pentalpha No.119

Continental Europe

Denmark

Forskningslogen Friederich Münter No.1 (Den Danske Frimurerorden)

United Grand Lodges of Germany

Quatuor Coronati Forschungsloge Nr.808
Located in Bayreuth; works in German language; researches German Freemasonry; Charter issued in 1951

American Canadian Grand Lodge within the United Grand Lodges of Germany

Past Masters Research Lodge No. 950
Located in Schweinfurt; works in English; research and education on the ritual used within the ACGL

National Grand Lodge of Greece

Lodge of Research Isis No. 9
Meets in Athens

Installed Masters No.18
Meets in Athens

Posseodonia No.44 (Provincial Grand Lodge of Piraeus and the Islands of the Aegean Archipelago)
Meets in Piraeus

Plato No.70
Meets in Athens

Grand Lodge of Iceland

Snorri No.14
Meets anywhere in Iceland

Regular Grand Lodge of Italy

The Lodge of Musical Research of the Regular Grand Lodge of Italy
Consecrated July 3rd, 2004

Pico della Mirandola Lodge No. 33 of Esoteric and Alchemical Research

Quatuor Coronati Lodge No. 112 of Historical Research
Consecrated April 5th, 1997

Quatuor Coronati No.1166 (Grand Orient of Italy)
In Perugia; Founded in 2000 by Palazzo Giustiniani; publishes books of Transactions, *Le Tavole* ("The Tables"), and has a correspondence "club" (CCQC) {website not available since before 7 June 2017}

Romania

Research Lodge Gnosis No.C3

Russia

Research Lodge Четверо Коронованных No.8 (Quator Quoronati)
Moscow

Sweden

Research and Education Lodge No.6 Aurora Borealis
Swedish Masonic Camp

Turkey

Mimar Sinan Lodge

Discovery Lodge of Research No.971 (United Grand Lodge of New South Wales and Australian Capital Territory)
Chartered in 1968

Western Australian Lodge of Research No. 277 (Grand Lodge of Antient Free & Accepted Masons of Western Australia)

Grand Lodge of Antient Free & Accepted Masons of South Australia and Northern Territory

Leichhardt No.225
Darwin

South Australian Lodge of Research No.216
Constituted October 8th, 1965 {website offline sometime before November 11th, 2013}

Grand Lodge of Tasmania

Hobart Lodge of Research No.62
Consecrated February 20th, 1948; caretakers of the Grand Lodge library and museum

Launceston No.69
Meets in Launceston

United Grand Lodge of Antient Free & Accepted Masons of Victoria

Holden Research Circle
Chartered in 1945

Victorian Lodge of Research No. 218

Grand Lodge of New Zealand

Hawke's Bay Research Lodge No.305

Masters' & Past Masters' Lodge No.130
Located in Christchurch

Midland District Lodge of Research
Meets at Timaru

The Research Lodge of Otago
Meets in Dunedin
{May be defunct}

Research Lodge of Ruapehu No.444
Located in Palmerston North

Research Lodge of Southland No.415
Meets at Invercargill

Top of the South Research Lodge
Meets in Nelson and other locations

Research Lodge of the Taranaki Province No.232
Meets in New Plymouth

United Masters Lodge
Meets in Auckland

The Waikato Lodge of Research

Research Lodge of Wellington
Meets in Petone

Asia

United Grand Lodge of England

The Lodge St. Michael No. 2933 E.C.
Singapore; Consecrated in 1902; "conducts Masonic research and provides resource facilities for all the Masonic Lodges in Singapore"

CHAPTERS, COUNCILS, AND PRIORIES

In recent years, concordant bodies have followed the model of Research Lodges, and share many of the same characteristics (detailed in the previous section). By default, they don't confer Degrees, they have presentations that may be published, and limit membership to those who are duly qualified, i.e. those who already received the Degrees of the tradition from a body recognized by their own grand body. The main difference is that they may focus on, or explore more deeply, those things that relate to the history and Degrees of their tradition.

Ohio Chapter of Research

Grand Chapter of Ohio, Royal Arch Masons, 1943

The Ohio Chapter of Research (OCR) was founded in 1943. Currently a period or revival, they are moving archives to the Chillicothe Masonic Temple from private storage and the Ohio Masonic Home campus.

The Edward M. Selby Award for Excellence in Masonic Research, instituted in 1990, is given out once per year but not every year.

Membership

Members may be from any recognized jurisdiction, but officers must be from their jurisdiction. The OCR went from 32 members to as many as 100 Active Members in the last few years, in part because free memberships were given to Chapter District Education Officers during their term of office.

Dr. William L. Cummings from Syracuse, NY, was awarded honorary membership on May 29th, 1948. There are currently no living honorary members.

Organizations can subscribe to publications.

Meetings

Meeting four times per year, they rotate meeting in different corners of the state from year to year. It's October meeting is held at its Grand Chapter Convocation.

Publications

The Chapter hasn't has a publication for nearly 20 years, previously having published their Transactions as a booklet or softcover book. They plan to put out one in 2025 to cover materials accumulated since that time. The OCR also is working to digitize and make prior proceedings available online.

Massachusetts Chapter of Research

Grand Royal Arch Chapter of Massachusetts, 1973

Massachusetts Chapter of Research (UD) was instituted September 22nd, 1973, "to diffuse Masonic light and knowledge; and to promote, encourage and conduct Capitular Masonic research". Like most Research Lodges, it does not confer Degrees, but has the usual elected and appointed officers. The group was defunct for a decade, but is now Under Dispensation. Its High Priest describes its activities as "friends getting together to explore what's possible".

It has undertaken efforts to convert Piers Vaughan's Capitular Development Course (developed for New York Royal Arch Masons) to be suitable for use in Massachusetts. .

Membership

Only Royal Arch Masons from Chapters of recognized jurisdictions may join. There are 72 Active Members. Dues are $20 per year with an application fee of $25. Dues are not being collected currently.

One honorary membership is given to a speaker each meeting, and can be from within or without the jurisdiction.

Any recognized Masonic body may be elected to subscribe to receive publications and links.

Meetings

Four Convocations per year are held with Royal Arch Research Chapters in Virginia, Ohio, Australia, and The Netherlands. The Fall convocation is in-person for installation with a festive board, modified for public attendance. The others are virtual, and Special Convocations may be held, invited by Masonic Temples within the state.

Publications

Publications are available through the Samuel Crocker Lawrence Library located at Grand Lodge in Boston. Transactions from 1973 through the 1990s are spiral-bound and are being converted to blog posts on the Grand Chapter's website and social media.

Virginia Research Royal Arch Chapter

Grand Chapter, Royal Arch Masons in Virginia

After years of consideration to form a Chapter for research in Virginia's Second Capitular District, Leonard M. Kilian and Bernard B. Belote, Jr. received permission from Grand High Priest Wilbur A. Buck to organize one. Modeling their by-laws after the Massachusetts Chapter of Research, they wrote a petition for dispensation similar to that of the A. Douglas Lodge of Research No.1949. It was presented at the Andrew Broady Capps, Jr. Royal Arch Ritual School held January 30th, 1984, in Norview. It contained 115 signers, and with the endorsement of the District Deputy Grand High Priest, was forwarded to the Grand Chapter. On March 30th, 1984, Grand High Priest Clyde William Rogers instituted the new entity as Virginia Research Royal Arch Chapter No.1753 (Under Dispensation), with 46 Companions present. Companion Kilian became the High Priest with Companion Belote as Secretary. The Charter was approved at the Grand Annual Convocation in October of that year, signed by Grand High Priest Frank Goodrich. The first Chapter of Research in the state, it was officially constituted

November 10th, 1984, in Chesapeake with 134 members and 35 petitions for affiliation.

A speakers bureau was set up in 1988 to provide programs for each Convocation.

Membership

No per capita is collected by the Chapter for its members.

Meetings

A Grand Chapter resolution exempts it from the requirement of monthly Convocations. Thereby, quarterly meetings are held, usually in Great Bridge, with the Annual Convocation being on the 3rd Saturday in September.

Thomas Smith Webb Chapter of Research

Grand Chapter State of New York Royal Arch Masons, 2002

The Thomas Smith Webb Chapter of Research was warranted on August 2nd, 2002, by the Grand Chapter, State of New York, Royal Arch Masons, making it the first (and only) Research Chapter in New York. It's purpose is "to encourage Royal Arch Masonic Research and study by its members and others, to present findings and conclusions to the Chapter for discussion and interchange, and to promote the discussion and debate of topics pertinent to Royal Arch Masonry".

Its founder and Honorary High Priest was Stephen A. Rubinstein. Inactive for nearly a decade, the Chapter was revived in 2022 by Past Grand High Priest (and Past Grand Master) Jeffery Williamson.

Membership

Membership is by affiliation only, as the Chapter does not confer Degrees. Any Royal Arch Mason of a Chapter in jurisdictions recognized by the Grand Chapter are eligible to be Active Members, who can vote and hold office. Corresponding Members can be any Royal Arch Mason or member of a Concordant Body recognized by The Grand Chapter. Individual Chapters, Grand Chapters, recognized Concordant bodies, Masonic research bodies, and libraries are also eligible. Annual dues are $20, with a petition fee of $25 which includes the first year's dues.

Fellowship is an honor conferred upon a Royal Arch Mason for outstanding achievement in Masonic research and publication, and Fellows can be proposed and accepted at any time. Currently only three Companions have been so honored: Grant Held; Oscar Alleyne; and Past Grand High Priest Piers Vaughan.

Meetings

The Chapter meets quarterly with occasional additional presentations, sometimes in conjunction with other bodies such as the American Lodge of Research, Ohio Lodge of Research, and the Western New York Lodge of Research. Typical locations include Albany, Utica (the home of the Masonic Campus), and at Grand Chapter, usually held in Binghamton in March.

Publications

In addition to an email newsletter, the Chapter has published two books of Transactions in 2010 and 2011, with eBook version available on LuLu.

Florida Chapter of Research

Grand Chapter of Royal Arch Masons of Florida, 2012

The Florida Chapter of Research was founded in 2012.

Membership

Currently at 47 members, they may be from any recognized jurisdiction. Officers must be from their jurisdiction.

Meetings

Meetings are held quarterly, with the location varying around the state. During the COVID-19 pandemic, meetings were virtual except at their annual meeting, which is done in conjunction with the Annual Meeting of the Grand York Rite of Florida.

Publications

They have an email newsletter.

Virginia Research Priory No.1823

Grand Commander William T. Hargrove established Virginia Research Priory No.1823 on April 27th, 2013, becoming the first Knights Templar Research Priory in the United States. Its purpose is "to perform research on the history, traditions, symbols, ritual, etc., of Chivalric Masonry in general and on Virginia Templary in particular and for its members to serve as a speaker's bureau for Constituent Commanderies of the Grand Commandery Knights Templar of Virginia".

Membership

Membership is open to all Sir Knights who hold membership under the Grand Encampment of the United States of America.

Enoch Council of Research

Grand Council of Indiana R. & S.M., 2021

The Enoch Council of Research (Under Dispensation) started in 2021. Notably, they resurrected the old rituals of the Knights of the Roundtable Degree and Knights of the Garter Degree. They now confer them with a Concordat established with the Grand Council of Indiana. Degree fees go to the Cryptic Masons Medical Research Foundation (CMMRF).

Membership

There are currently 21 members, and they may be from any recognized jurisdiction. Officers must be from their jurisdiction.

Organizations such as Lodges and libraries may subscribe to publications, of which there are currently five Corresponding Members.

Honorary membership is up to the will and pleasure of the Illustrious Master, based on various contributions to Cryptic Masonry and its research. At this time there is only one Honorary Member.

Meetings

Their dispensation allows them to meet elsewhere, but are domiciled in Auburn, meeting four times per year.

Publications

They are currently working on an academic publication, "The Emerald Tablet", a historical guide on early histories of the Degrees of Royal and Select Masters, as well as various esoteric topics. They are requesting open submissions, and funds raised by the sale of this publication will go to CMMRF.

They also have an email newsletter.

Florida Priory of Research

Grand Commandery of Knights Templar of Florida

The Florida Priory of Research was established on May 17th, 2021.

Membership

Official members may be from any recognized jurisdiction. Officers must be from their jurisdiction. They currently have 14 members.

Honorary Members may be from any recognized grand jurisdiction in amity with Grand Commandery of Florida.

Meetings

Quarterly meetings are held around the state or online. The Annual meeting is held with that of the Grand York Rite of Florida.

Publications

In addition to an email newsletter, they have done a circulation of presented papers to members.

RESEARCH SOCIETIES AND OTHER ORGANIZATIONS

With a few exceptions, Research Societies exist outside the framework (and authority) of the Grand Lodge system. They also tend to be more open to involvement by non-Masons, or Masons of unrecognized or Irregular nature, such as Universal Co-Masonry. Some are geographically tied to a state or region, while others are without borders.

The Masonic Service Association of North America

Though not strictly a research body, The Masonic Service Association of North America (MSANA), formerly named the Masonic Service Association, is an inter-jurisdictional body for relief and information.

Its original purpose was as a unified organization of Grand Lodges to aid military servicemen near the end of World War I, as the War Department declined working with the 49 Grand Lodges of the United States individually. The Grand Masters agreed to create it in 1918 at a gathering in Cedar Rapids, Michigan, and it was formally founded in 1919. Governed by a board of commissioners elected by various Masonic jurisdictions in North America, it provides "services to the Grand Lodges that they could not perform as easily individually" and plays a huge role in channeling disaster relief.

Their Short Talk Bulletins have been published monthly

since 1923 and are available in the following categories: Leadership; Entered Apprentice; Fellowcraft; Master Mason; About Individuals; Body of the Craft; Bypaths; Civic and Patriotic; Historical; Inspiration & Charity; In the Lodge Literature; Philosophy; Religion and Ethics; Symbols & Symbolism; The War and After. In brochure format, they can be purchased with a $12 per year subscription or individually for $2.00 each plus S&H. Finely-bound volume collections for various periods were printed, some being out of stock.

Their website, MSANA.com, contains statistics and other information regarding the jurisdictions in North America. They also have a Short Talk Bulletin Podcast and Short Talk Bulletin Online Audio Library.

The Philalethes Society

The Philalethes Society was founded by a group of Masonic authors on October 1st, 1928. The group was led by Founding President Cyrus Field Willard, Boston Globe reporter and founder of a Puget Sound commune for the group "Social Democracy of America". Willards stated that the group took its name, which is Greek for "lover of truth", from the Parisian Philalèthes.

Original members included Rudyard Kipling, Oswald Wirth, Robert I. Clegg, and J.S.M. Ward. Fellows (FPS) elected since that time include Carl H. Claudy (1936), Arthur Edward Waite (1937), Ray Denslow (1945), S. Brent Morris (1980), Norman Vincent Peale (1991), Jay Kinney (2010), Arturo de Hoyos (2014), W. Kirk MacNulty (2016), Mark A. Tabbert (2018), Andrew Hammer (2018), E. Oscar Alleyne (2018), Ric Berman (2018), and Robert L.D. Cooper (2018), as well as Paul M. Bessel and Elquemedo Oscar Allyne. A comprehensive list is available on their website.

The Certificate of Literature Award is given as "a just reward for literary and Masonic endeavor ... certified on the basis of worth, human interest and research". The most recent of these was given to Walter M. Macdougall in 2019 for "The Masonic Voyage Beyond: Bonded by Vision". They also award a Distinguished Service Medal.

In 1998, Allen E. Roberts published a book-length history of the Society, "Seekers of Truth".

Membership

In imitation of the Académie Française, membership is limited to 40, the requirement being a recognized Masonic author from any recognized Masonic jurisdiction.

Non-Masons and organizations can become part of the Correspondence Circle, and are referred to as "Members". These subscribers currently number about 1300, and receive publications, including an email newsletter.

Philalethes: The Review of Masonic Research and Letters

The first publication of its periodical was dated March 1946, edited by Walter A. Quincke. The delay in publishing their own works was due in part to the challenges of the Great Depression and World War II. Previous to this, its works appeared in other Masonic publications. Its earliest works were issued under the slogan "With

Rough Ashlar and Tracing Board" and motto "There is No Religion Higher than Truth".

Currently published quarterly, *Philalethes: The Review of Masonic Research and Letters* "has long served as the unofficial magazine for North American Freemasonry". The journal features "thought-provoking, substantial articles on Masonic symbolism, philosophy, ritual, artwork, literature and history" and is "carefully crafted to modern standards of design and scholarship" by its current editor, Shawn Eyer. The approach is to be "academically responsible, without being dry ... traditional, without stifling creativity and new ideas".

Events

The Society holds an Annual Assembly, where business is brought before it and reports are given by officers. All Members in good standing may vote. Attendees of Masonic Week may attend.

Society of Blue Friars

The Society of Blue Friars was formed in 1932 to recognize Masonic authors. According to Wallace McLeod,

> It is probably the smallest, and certainly one of the oddest, concordant bodies in Masonry. It has no fixed ritual or ceremonies, no dues or fees, and very few records. The name was chosen, presumably, because "Friar" is related to the French word for "Brother," and is therefore appropriate for a Masonic group; but it would also call to mind the monks of the Middle Ages, the ones who wrote most of the books in those days.

The Society has three officers: the Grand Abbot who presides for life or until stepping down; a Deputy Grand Abbot appointed by him to become his successor; and a Secretary-General. Its few regulations can only be changed by the Grand Abbott.

Membership

According to its few regulations, one new Friar is appointed each year, and the final decision is made by the Grand Abbot who receives nominations. Additional Friars "may be appointed to fill vacancies caused by demise or resignation when the total membership is not over twenty". There are no dues or fees of any kind.

Members include Arthur E. Waite (1939), Carl H. Claudy (1920). Ray V. Denslow (1937), S. Brent Morris (1998), Arturo de Hoyos (2000). Its 112th and newest member, added in 2024, is John W. Bizzack, "one of the driving forces behind the Rubicon Masonic Society".

Meetings

The Society meets once a year and has done so since 1944 except for in 1945. This "Consistory" is open to all Masons and is held as part of Masonic Week in Washington, D.C.. At this meeting, a new Friar is proclaimed and expected to deliver a research paper.

Publications

Papers were sometimes printed in the *Miscellanea* of the Allied Masonic Degrees, but more recently have appeared in *The Philalethes*. They may publish the collected Blue Friar Lectures at some point in the future.

Masonic Medical Research Institute

The Masonic Medical Research Institute (MMRI) is not strictly a Masonic Research body, but an "internationally recognized biomedical research institute" founded by the Grand Lodge of the State of New York. Over the years, it has been supported as a charity of choice by various Masonic jurisdictions.

Its story began when Past Grand Master Gay H. Brown founded the Masonic Foundation for Medical Research and Human Welfare, dedicated to research on rheumatic fever. Its first president was Past Grand Master Raymond C. Ellis. Groundbreaking for a facility was done on June 18th, 1955, its cornerstone was laid on April 7th, 1956, and was completed in June of 1958. In its first years, researchers discovered the cause of rheumatic fever and preventative procedures.

In the 1960s, a summer fellowship program, predoctoral and postdoctoral programs, and an experimental cardiology program were instituted. A wing funded by Royal

Arch Masons was added in 1974, and the foundation's name was changed to the Masonic Medical Research Laboratory" (MMRL) in 1976. The molecular biology program was started in the 1990s, where various discoveries were made in the area of cardiology, including "M" (for Masonic) cells and the gene responsible for sudden cardiac death. Brugada Syndrome was named in 1996 after Pedro and Josep Brugada, whose brother Roman Brugada became head of the department in 2002, around the time studies began on Sudden Infant Death (SIDS). The name and logo changed in recent years to reflect the expansion of its work and the genetic nature of much of its research.

During the COVID-19 pandemic, the MMRI conducted nearly 50,000 tests for the Mohawk Valley Health System.

The MMRI currently works in many areas in several laboratory teams. These include cardiac hypertrophy and heart failure, pulmonary embolism, metabolism and diabetes, lupus, autism, and electrophysiology. With funds from the Battle Within Foundation, a not-for-profit started by the Masons of Harmonie Lodge No.699 to bring awareness and help for veteran suicide, research is being done on possible genetic factors contributing to PTSD. Its mission statement today is

> To conduct high quality biomedical and clinical research aimed at generating knowledge and information necessary for understanding molecular

mechanisms of disease and development of medical cures and treatments of tomorrow. The Institute is also committed to providing education and training to basic scientists, clinical researchers and students who will perpetuate and extend the fight against disease worldwide.

Currently led by Executive Director Dr. Maria I. Kontaridis, there are currently over 50 employees representing a dozen countries. Over 50 scientific papers were published between 2018 and 2021. Its community service revenue, grants, and philanthropic gifts (Masonic and non-Masonic) totaled over $8 Million in 2020.

The MMRI also gives presentations to Lodges, and has Masons across the state act as ambassadors to bring awareness to what is considered one of the Jewels of their jurisdiction.

Masonic Book Club

Southern Masonic Jurisdiction, Ancient & Accepted Scottish Rite, 1970

The original Masonic Book Club (MBC) was founded in 1970 by Brothers Alphonse Cerza and Louis Williams of Illinois. Its primary purpose was reprinting out-of-print Masonic books, but also printed some original texts. It was first limited to 333 members, then opened to have at its peak almost 2000 members. In 2010, the Board of Directors decided to dissolve the Club and in 2017, with a membership still over 1000, the last of its assets were transferred to the Supreme Council of the Scottish Rite, Southern Masonic Jurisdiction.

According to their site, "The revived Masonic Book Club has the goals of publishing classic Masonic books and of supporting Scottish Rite SJ USA Philanthropies. Membership is open to anyone 18 years or older who is interested in the history of Freemasonry and allows you to purchase MBC editions at a pre-publication discount."

It is currently managed by S. Brent Morris, Past Grand Commander.

Membership

Membership is free and books are sold to benefit Southern Masonic Jurisdiction charities.

The Phylaxis Society

Brother Joseph A. Walkes, Jr., author of the book "Black Square and Compass", decided such a Lodge of Research ought to exist, but may not be easily understood and accepted within Grand Lodge, and needed to transcend the pleasure of any given Grand Master*. Using the organizational structure of the Philalethes Society – of which he was a member – as a guide, and living in one state while being a Mason in another, he set out to create a trans-jurisdictional body, one that was Afrocentric and "purely Prince Hall orientated". It is therefore not affiliated with any particular Grand Lodge or body.

He chose the name *Phylaxis* (Greek for "to watch or guard cautiously") and designed its logo based on that of the Philalethes Society, but added the number "15" to honor Prince Hall and the 14 others who were initiated with him. In 1970, he assembled officers – mostly fellow members of the military – from his worldwide Masonic travels.

Publishing the magazine became the goal. Bro. Allan G. Junier of the Tuskegee Institute in Alabama became its first editor, and many others within the group has extensive experience in writing and publishing, both Masonic and in the profane world. To draw the line against censorship from Grand Masters, he established its purpose: The Phylaxis Society was designed to create a bond of union for Prince Hall Masonic writers and also to protect editors of Masonic publications from undeserved aggression of some 'dressed in a little brief authority'". Letters were sent across jurisdictions announcing the creation of this new publication.

Volume 1 Number 1 of the Phylaxis magazine was issued in January 1974, the printing cost covered by Walkes himself. He writes, "With the mailing of this historic first issue, the entire hopes, dreams and aspirations of the Society went throughout Prince Hall Freemasonry and also to Caucasian Freemasons, and then the Society waited with silent prayer to learn how it was to be received."

Its website states more specifically that the Society "is partial toward dispersing light about Prince Hall and the network of masons that derive from The African Lodge of Boston, Massachusetts going back to 1775".

The Society is organized into chapters, where seven or more members request to be constituted as such. Around 40 chapters can be found across the United

States. Lux e Tenebris Research Chapter is unique in that it researches and publishes transactions on all aspects of Freemasonry, as well as critiques by its members.

A Council of Representatives functions as advocacy for the Society in various geographic regions. Related bodies include the York Rite Research Institute and Scottish Rite Institute.

Various honors are given by the Society, including the Jno. G. Lewis, Jr F.P.S. Medal of Excellence for "most outstanding Master Mason in Prince Hall Freemasonry". Others are awarded for articles written on Prince Hall Freemasonry by Prince Hall and other authors.

The Joseph A. Walkes, Jr. Commission on Bogus Masonic Practices

The mission of this initiative, organized by Brother Stephen Hill, FPS of California, is "to expose to the Prince Hall Freemason, Mainstream Freemason and the Public at Large those groups that cannot trace their lineage to African Lodge Number 459 or the United Grand Lodge of England, Ireland, or Scotland". Its purpose is also "to educate the innocent Bogus Mason of his origins". Its page on the Phylaxis website lists such clandestine groups and encourages people to report them, as well as provides information on court cases related to this issue.

Membership

Membership is open to those who first subscribe to the magazine. It is predominantly African-American, but any Mason from a jurisdiction recognized by the Prince Hall Conference of Grand Masters or the United Grand Lodge of England may become Active Members.

Events

A convention is held yearly.

Publications

Published up to four times per year, *Phylaxis* magazine "is the most respected and enduring international publication for Prince Hall Masons now extant". Back issues are available and sample articles are available on their website. Collections of its issues are available on Amazon.

Subscriptions to *Phylaxis* do not require membership and are available domestically (United States) and non-domestically for individuals and institutions. A lifetime option is available for domestic subscribers.

* Walkes suggests that Prince Hall Grand Masters have far more authority and tenure than in mainstream Grand

Lodges. His fear of having a Masonic organization taken over by such was mitigated by having its official address at a military base. It was noted on their website that A New York Prince Hall Masonic scholar, Harry A. Williamson, organized the first Lodge of Research in Prince Hall Freemasonry in 1943. It was chartered in New York for the purpose of promoting study and research, assist Brothers in the presentation of lectures, maintain a reference library, and issue an occasional book of its Transactions. It only published one volume, titled "PHLORONY" (acronym for "Prince Hall Lodge Of Research Of New York"). Awaiting a Charter it never received, the Grand Master, in January 1946, suspended the Lodge's work "for reasons never made known".

Maryland Masonic Research Society

Grand Lodge of Ancient Free & Accepted Masons of Maryland, 1979

The Maryland Masonic Research Society (MMRS) was founded in 1979 with the motto "Masonic Enlightenment through Research". It is not a Lodge, but provides Lodges educational ideas and topics for discussion.

Membership

Members are known as Companions and can be from recognized or unrecognized Obediences and even non-Masons, as "membership and officership are open to all who have an interest in Freemasonry". Dues are $35 per year and there are 72 members as of the writing of this entry. Members include Elwood E. Cook, S. Brent Morris, Ed Johnson, Walter Benesch, Cleola Bostic, Joi D. Grieg, Anne-Marie Moody (Grand Commander of Le Droit Humain, American Federation).

Lodges, libraries, and other organizations can subscribe to publications, being considered institutional members. All members have access to past and current research papers written by its members, and an online discussion forum.

Honorary Members include Past Presidents, Past Grand Masters, and Founding Members.

Meetings

There are at least four meetings per year and an annual Festive Board. They are held at various lodges in Maryland, but over Zoom during the COVID-19 pandemic. Since 2023, they do recorded hybrid in-person/virtual presentations.

Publications

In addition to their email newsletter, a repository of presentations are available in the member section of their website.

South Carolina Masonic Research Society

Most Worshipful Grand Lodge of Ancient Free Masons of South Carolina, 1988

Brethren from across South Carolina met in 1988 to discuss forming a study group. At the approval of Grand Lodge's Communication in April 1989, it's creation as the South Carolina Masonic Research Society (SCMRS) was affirmed "for the purpose of diffusing the true principles of Freemasonry by promoting, fostering, and conducting Masonic research and spreading Masonic knowledge". Though not a Lodge, it is subordinate to the Grand Lodge.

They "encourage lodges and other Masonic organizations to study their past and other aspects of their existence". Research is conducted by individual members on a variety of topics and are not limited to subjects related specifically to Freemasonry in the state. Their motto is "Light Through Knowledge".

Membership

Masons within the jurisdiction can become regular members. Masons from recognized jurisdictions can become Associate Members with the same rights and privileges except voting and holding office. Dues are $20 per year and entitle members to a copy of the yearly published Transactions. Life memberships are $300.

Lodges and organizations from recognized jurisdictions can become non-member subscribers to their publications.

Their by-laws provide for a class of membership styled "Fellow in Masonic Research (F.M.R)" for "meritorious service, exemplary conduct and/or exceptional and dedicated contribution to the Society".

Meetings

Conducted at various locations throughout the state by invitation of host Lodges, quarterly meetings are held in March, June, September, and December.

Publications

Their Transactions are published annually. The SCMRS

also makes available *Short Masonic Education Talks for The Lodge* free of charge. Each one has a Power Point and script.

The Scottish Research Society

Southern Masonic Jurisdiction, Ancient & Accepted Scottish Rite, 1991

The Scottish Rite Research Society (SRRS), formed in 1991 by S. Brent Morris and 13 others, received its charter from the Supreme Council, Southern Masonic Jurisdiction. It exists and works at the pleasure of the Grand Commander but is a separate legal entity. It's motto is "Studying our past to illuminate our future". It is governed by a Board of Directors, comprised of members representing Scottish Rite valleys across the country.

The Society presents two awards for "Excellence in Masonic Scholarship". The **Albert Gallatin Mackey Lifetime Achievement Award** is presented to "individuals whose works have received longstanding universal recognition by Masonic scholars", while the **Albert Gallatin Mackey Award for Excellence in Masonic Scholar-**

ship goes to "individuals whose original works published by the Society are distinguished by their superior achievement".

They are currently engaged in the "Order of the Royal Secret – Inspectors Information Project", looking for information regarding Inspectors and Deputy Inspectors. S. Brent Morris, Arturo de Hoyos, and Harold Van Buren Voorhis are acknowledged as contributors to this aspect of their history.

Donations go toward "defraying the costs of the collection, typesetting, printing, and storage of research materials and publications of the Society".

Membership

The Society now has over 4,000 members worldwide, and being a member of the Scottish Rite, or even a Mason, is not required. In addition to receiving its research journal, benefits include discounts on certain books and other items. Members also receive advance notice on important Masonic events. Memberships are $60 for residents or citizens of the United States and $95 for those in Canada and Mexico. Life memberships are also available.

Board members are life members.

Events

The Society originally met at regional Councils of Deliberation, but have no local meetings.

Publications

Their quarterly research journal, *The Plumbline*, focuses on research related to "Masonic history, philosophy, esoterica, customs, traditions, current interest commentary, and related subjects". It runs at around 3000 words, and openly accepts submissions.

Since 1992, "Heredom" has been the yearly hardcover publication of their Transactions, a tome similar to "Ars Quatuor Coronaturum" by Quatuor Coronati. It contains "a peerless collection of the finest and most thought-provoking essays on contemporary and historical Freemasonry, emphasizing the Scottish Rite". Back issues may be available at a reduced price.

Australia and New Zealand Masonic Research Council

The Australia and New Zealand Masonic Research Council (ANZMRC), established in 1992, "brings together the Masonic Research Lodges and Study Groups" across the seven Masonic jurisdictions of Australia and New Zealand.

A presentation by Tony Pope in 2007 laid out the Masonic research landscape at that time, showing that these jurisdiction permit or encourage Masonic Research. There are ten Research Lodges alone in New Zealand; South Australia & Northern Territory, Victoria, and Tasmania each have two; Western Australia, New South Wales & Australian Capital Territory, and Queensland each have one. There are also study groups, schools of instruction, and Lodges with interest in research. The earliest Research Lodges in Australia were established between 1889 and 1921.

It was Kent William Henderson, author of the "Masonic World Guide" (1984) and later Master of the Victorian Lodge of Research, who began contacting researchers to discuss his idea of a joint venture, namely to form an Australian Masonic Research Council. A constitution was quickly drafted, along with it's current aims, now worded as "Promote Masonic research and education; Act as a liaison body between its affiliated research lodges and chapters; Organise biennial conferences across New Zealand and Australia; Organise and coordinate Speaking tours by noted Masonic researchers; Publish the proceedings of its conferences and tour books of each touring speaker".

The organization was inaugurated at the first Conference of Australian Research Lodges in 1991. At this three-day event, the format for research papers was established. They are named the "Kellerman Lectures" in honor of Maurice Herman "Harry" Kellerman, OBE, founder of the Research Lodge of South Wales in 1968.

The Council was officially expanded to include New Zealand in 1996, adding half of the Lodges in that jurisdiction as members. During that same conference, the Council voted unanimously to admit the Phylaxis Society as an Associate Member, and present an award from that group to an Australian researcher. The following year began the publication of their quarterly journal.

Paul Bessel, Master of the Civil War Lodge of Research

in Virginia, attempted to form a similar council in the United States, but was unsuccessful.

Membership

Full Affiliate memberships with voting rights are available to Craft Research Lodges and informal research groups in Australia and New Zealand. Associate membership is non-voting and open to such groups elsewhere around the world. Affiliates and Associates receive a PDF version of the quarterly journal.

Since 2002, Fellows "whose contribution to the Council so merits" have been designated at conferences (limited to three or less per conference).

Events

A three-day conference is held every two years with multiple papers presented, mostly by speakers from Australia and New Zealand. The location is rotated around the States of Australia and the North and South Islands of New Zealand. Also every two years, the ANZMRC selects a well-known researcher and organizes a lecture tour across all its jurisdictions. The Council pays for travel expenses with reimbursement by visited Lodges. The papers presented during the tour is published afterward.

Publications

Harashim is the AMZMRC's quarterly Masonic research journal, the name meaning "Craftsman" in Hebrew. It contains "a variety of local and international news items, articles, book reviews, comments, research papers and other material". One may apply to receive it in PDF form by contacting the editor or may download past issues as annual volumes at their website or the website of the Linford Lodge of Research.

The ANZMRC's website also is the home of the Masonic Digital Library, containing over 5700 Masonic lectures, papers, and other material. Most of the content is restricted to members of participating organizations, and some content is by authors who are not members. Temporary access for evaluation may be granted on request.

Masonic Library and Museum Association

The Masonic Library and Museum Association (MLMA) is an independent, international organization "dedicated to preserving the history, literature, archives, and material culture of Freemasonry". They "bring the past to life through public education, research, and exhibits, while also supporting local lodges and organizations in their preservation efforts". It was formed in 1995 by a group of Masonic librarians and museum directors to "share their common experiences, interests and ideas".

Membership

Regular Members can be anyone who is interested in Masonic libraries and museums, such as Lodge Historians. Benefits include "receiving access to a full range of resources from around North America, invitations to programs and events, a list serve whereby one can ask the collective members about research related topics, and a digital newsletter".

Institutional Members are individuals who represent

"part of a professional organization (Grand Lodges, Lodges, Libraries, Museums, and other entities) that has a museums and/or library". As such they not only receive the regular member benefits, but may vote and hold office. Dues are $50 per year.

Publications

Various resources, such as newsletters and educational courses, are available to support those engaged in the preservation and handling of collections.

The Masonic Society

The Masonic Society is a "significant group of passionate Masons [who] have joined together to create what is now the fastest growing research society in Freemasonry". Members "have a deep and abiding desire to seek knowledge, explore history, discover symbolism, debate philosophies, and in short, who are at the forefront of charting a path for the future of Freemasonry". Their work includes extending assistance to, and working with, Research Lodges around the world. It provides an opportunity for such Lodges to have their papers published for an international audience.

Its name alludes to the Royal Society, the foundation of modern Western Science, which during the Age of Enlightenment was founded by many of the Masons who were influential in the formation of the first Grand Lodge. Founding members include Jeffrey M. Williamson, Past Grand Master of New York.

The Society works with the groups that put on Masonic Week, the Masonic Service Association, the Grand Encampment of Knights Templar of the United States, and the George Washington Masonic National Memorial Association. It also specially encourages research on topics related to York Rite Freemasonry.

Statewide and regional groups within the Society are

called "Second Circles", and organize local seminars, dinners, and other events.

Membership

The Society has members in 17 countries. Only Master Masons from certain recognized Grand Lodges can be members, namely those jurisdictions of the Conference of Grand Masters of Masons in North America (CGMMNA), or ones recognized by at least three of such Grand Lodges.

Dues are $45-67, depending on country, and each member receives a commemorative pin, patent of membership, and dues card. In virtue of their membership, members are eligible for discounts on items such as regalia, books, clothing, and jewelry. All members are automatically considered members of the regional Second Circles.

Subscribers pay the same rate as dues to receive the quarterly journal, and can be Non-Masons, Lodges, and libraries.

Honorary Fellows (FMS) are created by the Board of Directors bi-annually from among the membership "in recognition of outstanding contributions to the study of Freemasonry". Founding Fellows (2008) include Paul M. Bessel, Christopher L. Hodapp, S. Brent Morris, and Piers Vaughan. Subsequent Fellows include Andrew Hammer and E. Oscar Alleyne. A complete list is available on their website.

Events

The Society is an active participant of Masonic Week put on by the Allied Masonic Degrees, held each February in or near Alexandria, Virginia. This is where an annual "First Circle Gathering" is held, and another semi-annual symposium is held elsewhere.

Journal of The Masonic Society

Their quarterly journal, a full-color magazine titled *Journal of The Masonic Society*, "presents articles that enlighten our past, and explore solutions to the challenges facing Freemasonry today and tomorrow". It features content from well-known authors and everyday Masons alike. Research Lodges in particular are encouraged to submit content. The journal has advertising and publishes scholarship information from York Rite bodies.

The Masonic Philosophical Society

The Masonic Philosophical Society, founded in 2008, "seeks to recapture the spirit of the Renaissance that brought mankind so many scientific, artistic, and philosophical advancements without seeking to destroy spiritual pursuits". Its seal, an enneagram, is explained in detail on its website as a dedication to the destruction of ignorance. Topics of study include Natural Science, Behavioral Science, Formal Science, Philosophy, Theology, Esotericism, Art, Literature, and History, as well as their respective sub-disciplines.

Membership

Membership is free and open to Masons, Co-Masons, and non-Masons, "without distinction of race, age, sex, creed or religion". To become a member you must attest your sympathy with the "Three Grand Objects of The Masonic Philosophical Society: To destroy ignorance in all its forms; and to encourage the study of Culture, Philosophy, and Science; and to work for the Perfection of Humanity". There are currently 4,030 members.

Organizations can subscribe to publications.

Locations

The Society has Study Centers in 17 States and many other locations internationally, in countries speaking English, Spanish, Portuguese, and French, such as Brazil, Chile, Argentina, and Costa Rica. In addition to these centers, resources, speakers, and opportunities for dialogue are available online.

Publications

Members receive a monthly newsletter with information on events and activities at their various centers.

Boynton Lodge Esoteric Research Group

The Most Worshipful Grand Lodge of Free & Accepted Masons of Florida, 2010

Boynton Lodge Esoteric Research Group (BLERG) was formed in 2010 for the discussion of Freemasonry, Symbolism, Kabbalah, Tarot, Alchemy, and other topics.

Membership

Official members may be from any jurisdiction recognized by Florida, but corresponding members can be non-Masons. Currently there are 15 members and 40 corresponding members.

Meetings

Monthly meetings are held at Boynton Lodge in Boynton Beach, Florida. Several times a year, guest speakers have been brought in from around the world for more extensive seminars. These tyled, unrecorded presentations have included Robert L.D. Cooper, Martin Faulks, and Robert Davis. Fewer presentations were held during the COVID-19 pandemic, and future presentations may be available virtually.

The Rubicon Masonic Society

Grand Lodge of Kentucky, F.&A.M., 2013

The Rubicon Masonic Society was founded in 2013 and is headquartered in Lexington, Kentucky. It's purpose is to "assist in the improvement of one's self by establishing a deeper understanding of  Freemasonry, its traditions and practices, and further cementing the brotherhood of the Fraternity for the betterment of mankind".

According to their website, their members are "dedicated to the preservation of expressive fellowship as a means of transmitting wisdom, improving themselves, and the world around them".

> A goal of the Society is the cementing of brotherhood in support of the inner transformation of each individual on the path toward self-mastery. The Society views the improvement of the individual as the most fundamental aspect of improving society.

Suitable topics for well-researched papers include Masonic symbolism, history, philosophy, and "the spiritual path of self-transformation in the pursuit of virtue".

Membership

Official, full members may be from any recognized jurisdiction and currently number around 15 in addition to honorary members. Full Members are expected to inform another Member or the Secretary of the Society if they will be absent.

Organizations may subscribe to publications.

Meetings

Masons of all Degrees from any Grand Lodge recognized by Kentucky are welcome to attend. Non-Masons who are vouched for as considering joining the Fraternity may also attend. These are not tyled and the attire is a coat and tie. Drinking, smoking, and foul language are strictly prohibited. An open discussion period follows presentations. Live Virtual Education is held on the evening of the last Monday of each month. The Society makes it clear that these are not a substitute for Lodge meetings. Members-only meetings are via private dinners.

Publications

In addition to an email newsletter, recordings of video presentations are also available to members. Monthly Masonic education can be found on their YouTube Channel. "The Masonic Table Documentary" is available for rent online. Their first hardcover Transactions, "The Rubicon Masonic Society Transactions Vol. 1" was published in 2023 and is available on Amazon.

Masonic Research Network

The Masonic Research Network (MRN) in Iowa was created in 2013, "[i]n response to a long-standing and growing need for, and a renewed interest in the esoteric, philosophical and symbolic teachings of Masonry among the Craft". Sponsored by the Sioux City Valley of the Ancient and Accepted Scottish Rite (Southern Jurisdiction), it is an independent entity, not associated with the Grand Lodge of Iowa or the Scottish Rite.

According to an archived version of its website,

> Iowa Freemasonry has long been preeminent in Masonic education, it being the home of The National Masonic Research Society (1915 – 1932), the Masonic Service Association of North America (1918 – Present), the Iowa Academy of Masonic Knowledge (2013 – Present) and the Grand Lodge of Iowa Library located in Cedar Rapids, Iowa.

{Their website went dark sometime on or before January 2022 and is unclear if the MRN still exists or is active.}

Membership

Membership is free, made by creating an account on their website's discussion forum. By using it, one attests they are a "Qualified Brother Master Mason".

The website forum was a repository Masonic publications on various subjects, such as "Symbolism & Philosophy, Law & Jurisprudence, Masonic History, Masonic Leadership, Lodge Activities", as well as article and book reviews, quizzes, a photo gallery, and threaded discussions.

The Masonic Formation Academy

The Masonic Formation Academy (MFA), founded in 2020 by academician Shawn Byer, is "not a research society as such but an educational body using live discussions" and "to provide a range of in-depth Masonic education experiences". It offers long-form online seminars, the most popular of which is the "Early Texts of Freemasonry Seminar Series" (ETFM). These are "private, cohort-based, open-duration e-learning" using a graduate-level discussion format.

Membership

Official members may be from any recognized jurisdiction and the Academy currently has 85 members. Different levels of monthly membership tuition are available through Patreon.

Meetings

The MFA holds weekly, virtual, one-hour discussions, where "[m]anuscripts, catechisms, lectures, constitutions, songs, ceremonies, and sermons are examined with the purpose of making the beliefs and ideas of the early Freemasons accessible".

Mabini Society for Nationhood

The Mabini Society for Nationhood (MSN) was incorporated on December 27th, 2020, the Feast of St. John the Evangelist. It is "an international learned society for the study of fraternalism in Philippine Society and the

contributions of Freemasonry to the Filipino Nation". It is not under the Grand Lodge of the Philippines, but us in process of getting a memorandum of understanding.

It was founded in part because the Philippine Lodge of Research was seen as inactive and that a society may play a role in education that extends the the general public. Patriotic in nature, it is named for Apolinario Mabini, revolutionary leader and first Prime Minister of the Philippines. Some don't consider it to be Masonic because of its inclusivity and lack of specifically Masonic work.

Membership

Masons under the Grand Lodge of the Philippines, as

well as non-Masons, may join so long as they are not Irregular. There are currently 45 official, full members. They are in the process of establishing what are Fellows.

Organizations may be sponsors, engage in joint activities, and be donors.

Meetings

Meetings are held quarterly, in English & Filipino, at the conference room at Grand Lodge (Teodoro Kalaw Memorial Chamber) in Manila.

Publications

The Society holds recorded video presentations and webinars, and may eventually publish a journal. Papers are citation-based using any style.

ONLINE RESOURCES

Masonic Websites

There are countless websites about Freemasonry. Some have stood the test of time or have become regularly used sources of information. The author has included the ones that seem to be the most prominent and of general usefulness to the Craft, along with a few lesser-known sites that may be of interest to the reader.

Paul Bessel

Paul M. Bessel's website, **Bessel.Org**, was a collection of information related to Freemasonry. It contained over 200 web pages on topics ranging from information on Grand Lodge jurisdictions and recognition to historical and patriotic topics, particularly related to the District of Columbia. Started sometime in 1998, it became a long-standing reference and repository. {*The author of this book referenced it often, especially "What Happened on this Date in Masonic History".*}

The site was down over two months at the turn of 2017, and the Masonic Society worked with him to restore it. By that time, it was already an inactive archive. Sometime on or before September 2014, his site had an added footnote: "Please note that I no longer am updating the webpages about Freemasonry. I still maintain my memberships but otherwise I am not active." It went dark sometime in 2023. However, a permanent record of it can be found using the Wayback Machine on Archive.Org. The archives are in the process of being recreated by the Masonic Digital Trust, and any request to terminate the project will be respected if there is a lawful claim or objection.

Brother Bessel was born January 24th, 1949, in Brooklyn, New York. He was a lawyer, was married, and lived in Silver Spring, Maryland, having visited "all United States except Idaho, Wyoming, and North and South Dakota". His Masonic memberships include that of numerous Lodges, mostly in the District of Columbia, but also Zeredatha Lodge No.483 in Brooklyn and Bannack Historical Lodge in Montana. A Past Senior Grand Warden of the Grand Lodge of Washington DC, he was also an Honorary Junior Grand Warden of the National Grand Lodge of France and an Honorary Senior Grand Deacon in the Grand Lodge of Armenia.

His positions with Research-related bodies include: President of the Masonic Library & Museum Association from 1999 to 2001; Librarian of the George Washington Masonic National Memorial, from 1995 to 2002; Fellow and Life Member of the Philalethes Society; Fellow and Life Member of the Scottish Rite Research Society; Fellow of The Masonic Society; Fellow of the Maine Lodge of Research; and James R. Case Fellow of the Connecticut Lodge of Research.

His articles have been published in *The Philalethes*, the *Scottish Rite Journal*, *Heredom*, *The Plumbline*, *The Phylaxis*, and other Masonic publications. He was also the author of "Masonic Questions & Answers" (Cornerstone Publishers, 2005) and "Out of the Shadows: The Emergence of Prince Hall Freemasonry in America, 200 Years of Endurance", co-authored with Alton G. Roundtree (KLR Publishing, 2006).

{Brother Bessel is no longer active in Masonic organizations and his exact circumstances are unknown.}

Grand Lodge of British Columbia & Yukon

The Grand Lodge of British Columbia & Yukon, found online at **Freemasonry.BCY.CA** features comprehensive content about Freemasonry and also addresses anti-Masonic rhetoric. It has sections for general information, biographies, papers and essays, and further information. It also features music, regalia, jewelry, and other items. The site map lays out all the content in outline form.

This work is attributed to Trevor McKeown.

Craftsmen Online

CraftsmenOnline.Com was started during the COVID-19 pandemic by Grand Master Steven Adam Rubin and Brother Michael Arce, the host of The Craftsmen Online Podcast with 25 years experience in radio broadcasting. A semi-official channel of the Grand Lodge of the State of New York, their goal is "to produce Masonic content that focus on Education, History, Leadership, and the Membership Experience". The podcast airs every Monday morning, there is a reading room program, and the website features sections on art and history.

Other team members include: Brother Bill Edwards, member of Philalethes Society, Masonic Society, and an Associate Member of the Lodge of the Living Stones in Leeds; Samuel Lloyd Kinsey; Michael LaRocco, and Director of the Chancellor Robert R Livingston Masonic Library; Bro. Okbani; Todd M. Paterek; Anthony Prizzia; Asly Raymond; Ronald J. Seifried, author of "Long Island Freemasons" (Arcadia Publishing, 2020); and Jason W. Short.

Anyone may subscribe to email updates.

Emeth

Emeth.Substack.Com is the blog and podcast of Cameron M. Bailey, Past Grand Master of The Most Worshipful Grand Lodge of Free & Accepted Masons of Washington. Emeth, meaning "truth" in Hebrew, is an almost daily email newsletter and web archive of essays and discussion topics of interest to Masons, with a focus on improving the Lodge experience. In his words,

> By learning together and reimagining Freemasonry, we can create Legendary Lodges, Legendary Brotherhood. Legendary Freemasonry. We can Live this Legend, and by doing so we will grow and inspire our Ancient Craft.

With thousands of visitors each week, subscribers get additional exclusive content and access to live discussions via Zoom.

Freemasons for Dummies

The site **FreemasonsForDummies.blogspot.com** is the "world's most popular Masonic news blog site". It is the work of Christopher L. Hodapp, author of the worldwide best-selling book "Freemasons For Dummies" and current President of the Masonic Library and Museum of Indiana. With an extensive involvement in Grand Lodge, Scottish Rite, and even a Templar period recreation degree team, he is a member, officer, or honorary member of numerous Lodges and bodies, and has received various Masonic awards. Having written "Solomon's Builders: Freemasons, Founding Fathers, and the Secrets of Washington, D.C." and and co-authored "The Templar Code For Dummies and Conspiracy Theories and Secret Societies For Dummies", he was inducted into the Society of Blue Friars for Masonic authors.

FreemasonInformation.Com

FreemasonInformation.Com features itself as the "Freemason Information Digital Masonic Magazine". Its tagline is "The future of Freemasonry rests in the knowledge of the past". It has well-organized, comprehensive information on general knowledge and how to become a Freemason. According to the site, it is "entirely independently operated and supported out of a passion for the fraternity" and "exists to broaden the understanding of non-Masons who have an interest in the fraternity". It serves as a broad overview of Masonry and its place in society rather than speaking from the perspective of a particular Grand Lodge. A free eBook, "What is Freremasonry", can be downloaded free from the site.

Masonic Information is led by Gregory B. Stewart with contributions by Fred Milliken and Tim Bryce.

{*Author's Note: Their website is one of the few reviewed here that has a fully mobile-responsive, modern design. The author recommends it as an example to aspire to for other Masonic information sites.*}

Freemasonry Network

Freemasonry.Network was created by in 2018 by "the enthusiasm of a few gathered Brethren" from the United States and Poland. It boasts that it is now "one of the largest Internet portals devoted to Freemasonry in the world". It features information on various aspects of Freemasonry, such as its various bodies, anti-Masonry, and Freemasonry's relation to society, science, and deity. Over 1,000 videos and hundreds of links on these subjects are available on the site. The content includes

information and news on "Liberal" Freemasonry (Irregular jurisdictions, including Women's Lodges and Co-Masonry). Member-only content is available through a Patreon subscription.

The site features almost daily news articles on Masonic events and issues around the world. Having created "the largest news service relating to the United Grand Lodge of England and its Provincial Grand Lodges", they also work with popular American Masonic portals and podcasts. Their goal is become the world's first "fully professional news service" devoted to Freemasonry.

They are also the main promoter of the "Enough is Enough" Campaign, an effort to influence the perception of Freemasonry in news media and online. This is in part to combat what the United Grand Lodge of England describes as members being "victims of gross misrepresentation and discrimination". It does this by "regularly publishing information aimed at creating a positive image of Freemasonry".

It's current editor-in-chief is Klaus Dąbrowski, author of "100 Freemasons" and "Freemasons: 555 Illustrations".

MasonicInfo.Com

Edward L. King's site, **MasonicInfo.Com**, focuses on apologetics, addressing Masonic myths and anti-Masonic propaganda. It contains "over 370 pages of facts" dealing with everything from the Illuminati and Lucifer to the DaVinci Code and clandestine groups. One of the most recent featured articles is documentation and discussion regarding false claims that President Obama is a Freemason. There is also positive content that talks about actual Masonic organizations, activities and how to join.

It also features a tongue-in-cheek link to "Toys-R-Us" in a statement to readers that "if you're absolutely sure that Masonry is wrong and you know this beyond a shadow of doubt, click here and go directly to some things especially for you!"

{*Caveat: This site may no longer be maintained, as the design is archaic, likely from its creation in 1998, and its copyright notice only extends to 2014.*}

The Magpie Mason

At **TheMagpieMason.blogspot.com**, New York Mason Jay Hochberg has written innumerable articles on the Craft since 2008. He describes himself as "an obscure journalist in the Craft who writes, with occasional flashes of superficial cleverness, about Freemasonry's current events and history; literature and art; philosophy and pipe smoking".

Brother Hochberg is Worshipful Master of the American
Lodge Of Research, Past Master of New Jersey Lodge of
Masonic Research and Education 1786, past president of the
Masonic Society, and a member of Virginia's Civil War
Lodge of Research No.1865.

Masonic Digital Trust

The site **MasonicDigitalTrust.org** is a project for long-
term support of Lodge digital assets and records, as well
as website development and hosting. It is the offshoot of
the author's company, **Kentropolis.Com**. It also contains
information on the concept model of "Digital Square
Clubs" for Masons who want to network in their service
to the craft respecting digital art and communication.

Masonic Speakers Association

Associated with WCY (Whence Came You) Media,
MasonicInstruction.Com is a listing of over 60 speakers,
with their respective biographies, topics, and conditions
to arrange engagements. A contact form is available for
each.

The list includes: Randy Sanders, founder of Refracted Light; author Christopher Earnshaw, Past Master of the Research Lodge, Grand Lodge of Japan; author Tim Hogan; Ken JP Stuczynski (author of this book), and Kathleen Aldworth Foster, author of the book of historical fiction, "Doneraile Court: The Story of The Lady Freemason".

The Midnight Freemasons

The blog at **MidnightFreemasons.Org** is an informal group of Master Masons run by Darin A. Lahners and Managing Editor Robert "RJ" Johnson. Contributors write "each from their own unique perspective" on various subjects related to Freemasonry, including "history, trivia, travel, book reviews, great quotes, and hopefully a little humor as well".

In addition to Borthers Lahners and Johnson, contributing authors include Todd E. Creason, 33°, Gregory J. Knott, 33°, Randy Sanders, Ken JP Stuczynski, Patrick M. Dey, Jim Stapleton, Phillip Welshans, and Erik M. Geehern.

The Phoenixmasonry Masonic Museum and Library

Phoenixmasonry.Org is the home of The Phoenixmasonry Masonic Museum and Library. It's tagline is "An Independent and Universal Masonic Resource" and describes its importance to "Phoenixmasons" ("e-Masons") as a "well-kept repository of … treasured Masonic heritage and humble origins". It founder and president, David J. Lettelier, describes its mission as "dedicated to facilitating a spiritual rebirth and resurrection in the philosophy of Freemasonry".

A 501(c) corporation based in Colorado, it's mission statement reads:

> We believe that faith in God gives meaning and purpose to human life; that Masonry was, "the original network," of like-minded men who united in a common cause to share their opinions and work together on constructive projects. Now to complete this evolution, it must be transferred on a global scale to the internet. The designs upon our electronic trestle boards will promote research and education and advance our historical foundation and rich cultural heritage. Our mission is to clarify the present through appreciation of the past.
>
> We believe that Freemasonry recognizes that times do change and we must grow with them. Our roots are firmly planted in the Renaissance of the Dark Ages, but its branches extend into the future. That future is one of technology, science, literature and music and is a course we as Phoenixmasons (e-Masons) are committed to shine "further Light" upon. We believe in those solemn obligations taken at our sacred altar to provide for the less fortunate, exemplify patriotism, and perform the duties of citizenship. Now, let us enjoy true fellowship attending this electronic educational resource while practicing its principles, tenets and beliefs; ever-remembering that it is the shared synergy of Brotherly Love and affection that heals us both physically and spiritually.

There are countless pages and on every Masonic subject imaginable, and pages devoted to individual artifacts of all kinds. Myriad links take users to videos, including captures of the "Fran Foster's Masonic TV Show". There is also a "marketplace" of links to Masonic items that can be purchased from various sources and craftsmen. It's

YouTube Channel featured it's own show at one time, the most recent being in 2020. Brother Frederic L. Milliken was the Executive Director for Phoenixmasonry as of 2018.

A most notable feature is public access to ritual texts, similar to what can be found at Sacred-Texts.Com.

{*Even though the site design is archaic, probably similar to its creation in 1999, the copyright notice extends to 2019, and there are links to affiliated channels on Facebook, Pinterest, Instagram, YouTube, Twitter (X), Google+, reddit, and Tumblr. These channels appear to be actively maintained.*}

The Quarry Project

The Quarry Project is a workshop sponsored by The Masonic Society and the Masonic Library and Museum Association, starting with a conference in 2013 on Masonic research and preservation. According to its website,

> [It] drew from both the Masonic and academic communities to provide detailed instruction on Masonic research and the editing of the results. Additionally, a set of voluntary standards for future

Masonic research, writing, and editing were introduced. Professional librarians, museum curators, and experts on display and preservation provided practical instruction and advice on maintaining and improving Masonic historical repositories.

Found at **TheQuarryProject.Com**, their style guide is used in many jurisdictions and the publications of various Masonic organizations.

Phase II of their project is in the works, and their site will be updated regarding their "next step" for Masonic historians, archivists, and researchers.

YorkRite.Org

Since August 25th, 1997, Brother Dan Pushee has developed and maintained what is now **YorkRite.Org**, a compendium of information on York Rite bodies and events around the world with over 1500 links. He is a member, and was often an officer, leader, honorary member, or otherwise honored by over 50 Masonic Lodges and bodies. He currently works as webmaster of dozens of York Rite Grand Bodies and other Masonic organizations. In recent years, Brother Ken Stuczynski (the author of this book and a professional web developer) has assisted Dan in modernizing and hosting these sites.

Sources and Notes

The following are the sources used for each of the individual entries in this book.

Some of these, and most of the ones listed under "Other Lodges", do not have current information online and such was obtained by using archived versions of the web pages on <u>Archive.Org</u>. Many have social media profiles that are maintained as of the writing of this book (through which the author requested information); others may be defunct or inactive.

Lodges

Quatuor Coronati
Interview with S. Brent Morris, September 7th, 2021; <u>QuatuorCoronati.Com</u>; "Ars Quatuor Coronatorum, Vol. 133"; corresponding letter; QC Correspondence Circle email, October 5th, 2020

Lodge of Research No.2429
<u>Research2429.org.uk</u>

Jubilee Masters Lodge
<u>JubileeMastersLodge.wordpress.com</u>

Barron Barnett Lodge
<u>BarronBarnett.org.au</u> {archived October 24, 2023}

Lodge of Research No.CC
homepage.eircom.net/~minoan/Lodge200

American Lodge of Research
ALRNY.org

Walter F. Meier Lodge of Research
WalterFMeier.com

Research Lodge of Oregon
Research198.Org; facebook.com/ResearchLodgeOfOre-gonNo198

Northern California Research Lodge
NCRL.Freemason.org

Philosophic Lodge of Research Lodge
lodgelocator.com/philosophic-lodge-of-research-400

Missouri Lodge of Research
MOLOR.Org;

Virginia Research Lodge
Interview with Christopher W. Douglas, Oct 9th, 2021, currently the Junior Deacon and key person in the preservation of papers in existing and past Lodges and bodies of research in Virginia; facebook.com/groups/researchlodge

Southern California Research Lodge
TheResearchLodge.com

Research Lodge of Colorado
Correspondence with Vic Ament, Past Master; www.rlcolo.org

Texas Lodge of Research
Texas Lodge of Research.Org; interview with Truitt Bradly, Secretary

Anniversary Lodge of Research
AnniversaryLodge.org; Mark Langis

Linford Lodge of Research
LinfordResearch.info; Neil Morse

William O. Ware Lodge of Research
WilliamOWareLodgeOfResearch.com; correspondence with Orlando dos Santos

Ohio Research Lodge
lor.clubexpress.com; document annotated as OLR 5 (1997-2003); Jeff Slattery, Past Master

Masonic Lodge of Research
lodgelocator.com/masonic-lodge-of-research-401

The Oklahoma Lodge of Research
OklahomaLodgeOfResearch.com; Daniel Hanttula

Georgia Lodge of Research
www.kennesaw33.net/georgia-lodge-of-research-1.html

Florida Lodge of Research No.999
grandlodgefl.com/glf-education/florida-lodge-of-research/; facebook.com/FLR999/; Flor999.com (archived September 23, 2023); Richard Lynn, Past Grand Master & Grand Secretary; Scott Schwartzberg

Illinois Lodge of Research
IllinoisLodgeOfResearch.org; Victor Williams

The Heritage Lodge
HeritageLodge730.com

Nevada Lodge of Research
NLOR2.org; Michael Kurcab

Maine Lodge of Research
mainemason.org/uploads/MLR_Brochure_1.pdf; maine-lodge-of-research-me.ourlodgepage.com; mainelodgeofresearch.com {archived February 5th, 2023}

A. Douglas Smith, Jr. Lodge of Research
ADSLoR.Org

Eastern Washington Lodge of Research
MW Cameron Bailey; Merle Iverson

Western New York Lodge of Research No.9007
Western New York Lodge of Research Books of Transactions 1983-2013; WNYLodgeOfResearch.US; personal knowledge of author

Ted Adams Lodge of Research
facebook.com/TedAdamsLodgeofResearch998; *Lodges of Research*, presented by Dan M. Kemble, Master, William O. Ware Lodge of Research, February 19th, 2019.

Tennessee Lodge of Research
TNLoR.org {archived April 14, 2024}

Ted Adams Lodge of Research
Ethan Weles, Secretary

Silas H. Shepherd Lodge of Research
lulu.com/spotlight/silashshepherd; Groupable Connect

Dwight L. Smith Lodge of Research U.D.
DLSLodgeOfResearch.net

Louisiana Lodge of Research
lalodgeofresearch.org; Brandon Smith

Research Lodge of the Grand Lodge of Japan
Interview with Dr. Christopher Earnshaw, January 24, 2022 (JST), a Master of the Lodge for three years and Past Grand historian for the Grand Lodge of Japan.

Infinity Lodge of Study and Research
RW Carl J. Klossner

Temple of Athene Lodge
MiddlesexFreemasons.org.uk/temple-of-athene/

Civil War Lodge of Research
CWLR.org; Bennett Hart, Past Master

Justice Robert H Jackson Lodge of Study and Research
Jim Stoll; Tom Nelson

Edward J. Wildblood Jr. Dermont Vermont Lodge of Research
VermontLodgeOfResearch.com

Internet Lodge of Research
InternetLodge.ab.ca; Bill Thomas, member and Past Grand Master of New York

Pennsylvania Lodge of Research
PALodgeOfResearch.org; A *History of The Pennsylvania Lodge of Research* No. 11 by Paul D. Fisher, Past Master and Fellow, edited and revised by Christopher D. Rodkey, Worshipful Master

New Jersey Lodge of Masonic Research & Education
NJLoRE1786.com

The James M. Simms Lodge of Research
jsnow1.tripod.com/jmslorga.htm

Forskningslogen Niels Treschow
frimurer.no/loger/forskningslogen; frimurer.no/loger/forskningslogen/forskningslogen-niels-treschow-av-br-kurt-ringstad; Leif Endre Grutle

Massachusetts Lodge of Research
MALodgeOfResearch.org;

Mississippi Lodge of Research and Education
Terry McLeod; former site MSLodgeOfResearch.org {archived June 3rd, 2023}

Alabama Lodge Of Research
AlabamaLodgeOfResearch.org {archived November 19th, 2015}; *Alabama Freemasons* Vol. I, Issue I (December 2010); MYALoR.org, archived December 5th, 2025 (under reconstruction)

George Washington Lodge of Research No. 1732
GWLodge.org; Shelby Chandler

COLLEGIUM LVMINOSVM Lodge of Research
CollegivmLvminosvm.org; interview with David Lavery on August 5th, 2023

Lebanon Research Lodge
Interview with founding Worshipful Master, February 18th, 2022

Other Research Bodies

Ohio Chapter of Research
OhioChapterOfResearch.org; S. Jefferson Slattery, High Priest

Massachusetts Chapter of Research (UD)
MAYorkRite.site/research; MAYorkRite.site/grand-

chapter/9-grand-chapter/67-chapter-of-research (old page with more detail); Bryan Simmons, High Priest, May 2nd, 2022

Virginia Research Royal Arch Chapter No.1753
Presentation by Leonard M. Kilian and Bernard B. Belote, Jr., September 16, 1989

Thomas Smith Webb Chapter of Research
Personal information of author, who is currently serving as King; old literature and website, now TSW.NYRAM.Org

Florida Chapter of Research
Joshua Schutts; Scott Schwartzberg

Virginia Research Priory No.1823
www.travelingtemplar.com/2013/05/virginia-research-priory-1823.html

Enoch Council of Research U.D.
Michael Doxsee

Florida Priory of Research
Joshua Schutts; Scott Schwartzberg

Masonic Research Societies and Other Organizations

The Masonic Service Association of North America
MSANA.Com

The Philalethes Society
Freemasonry.org; philalethes.myshopify.com;
en.wikipedia.org/wiki/Philalethes_Society; Shawn
Eyer and Tyler Vanice

The Society of Blue Friars
mwsite.org/sbf/; www.travelingtemplar.com/2014/07/
the-society-of-blue-friars.html; myfreemasonry.com/
threads/masonic-week-2024-john-bizzack-
named-112th-blue-friar.32332

Masonic Medical Research Institute
MMRI.edu

Masonic Book Club
ScottishRite.org/media-publications/masonic-book-
club/

The Phylaxis Society
ThePhylaxis.org

Maryland Masonic Research Society
MD-MRS.com; Cleola Bostic

South Carolina Masonic Research Society
scmrs.org {archived December 7th, 2023}

The Scottish Research Society
ScottishRiteResearch.com; *Northern Light* magazine,
August 2021

Australia and New Zealand Masonic Research Council

(ANZMRC)
ANZMRC.org; linfordresearch.info/anzmrc-newsletters-harashim

Masonic Library and Museum Association
Masonic-Libraries.com

The Masonic Society
TheMasonicSociety.com

The Masonic Philosophical Society
PhilosophicalSociety.org; Matias Cumsille

Boynton Lodge Esoteric Research Group
Scott Schwartzberg

The Rubicon Masonic Society
RubiconMasonicSociety.com; Brian Evans

Masonic Research Network
Former site, ResearchMasonry.com {archived August 4th, 2021}

The Masonic Formation Academy
Facebook.com/masonicformation; Shawn Eyer

Mabini Society for Nationhood
Interview with Teodoro Kalaw IV, August 8-9th, 2023, the son and grandson of Past Grand Masters including Teodoro Kalaw, whose Memorial Chamber is the meeting place of the Society.

About the Author

Brother Ken JP Stuczynski hails from the Grand Lodge of the State of New York, raised in West Seneca Lodge No.1111. He currently sits as Master of Western New York Lodge of Research No.9007 and King for the Thomas Smith Web Royal Arch Chapter of Research. He is a 32nd Degree Scottish Rite Past Sovereign Prince of the Valley of Buffalo, past High Priest of East Aurora Royal Arch Chapter No.282, and Patron of Pond Chapter No.853 Order of the Eastern Star. He currently serves as Assistant Grand Lecturer of the Erie District of New York, District Grand Lecturer of the Erie District of the Order of the Eastern Star, and Educational Officer for the 16th Capitular District of Royal Arch Masons.

Brother Ken is a regularly published Masonic author on topics from technology and futurism to history and esotericism. Many of his articles have appeared in *Empire State Mason* magazine and *Midnight Freemasons*. In addition to editing and publishing the Transactions of the WNY Lodge of Research (under the *cyphrGlyffe* imprint of his company, Amorphous Publishing Guild), he is author of "Webmastering the Craft: Fraternity in a Digital World" (2020).

Professionally, he owns Kentropolis Internet, a webhosting and development company providing web services for companies, community organizations, and individuals for over 25 years. Under the brand Masonic Digital Trust, it provides services to over a hundred Masonic organizations, including hosting and support for MW Sites by Dan Pushee. He has been webmaster of NYMasons.Org (Grand Lodge of New York) and NYRAM.Org (New York's Royal Arch Grand Chapter) for over ten years.

Most importantly, Ken lives a happy life with his wife and numerous pets in South Buffalo, fully content with his early life choice to get a degree in Philosophy.

To learn more about Ken,
follow, or receive his newsletter, visit

KenVille.Net

WEBMASTERING THE CRAFT

Fraternity in a Digital World

Bro. Ken JP Stuczynski
2020 Edition

Also by the Author: A guide for Masonic and other fraternal organizations to navigate the modern world of communications and information. Covers modern communication and public relations methods and strategies as well as organizational considerations. Contains guidance on websites, social media, the cloud, conferencing and collaboration tools. Bonus material: Twenty short articles advocating technology and its role in Freemasonry. Available worldwide.